The Christian life is shaped by testimonies of how God is at work in our lives–saving us, leading us; oftentimes, leading us through shadowed valleys. Danny and Cynthia share their testimonies of lives lived in service of churches and Christian institutions that ultimately failed to live up to the command Jesus gave us—to love our neighbors as ourselves. They call us to the hard but healing road of living the truth in love.

Megan K. DeFranza, PhD, author of
Sex Difference in Christian Theology: Male, Female, and Intersex in the Image of God

Intersexion is like and unlike any book I have read. Like, in that it includes three genres that are growing today—memoirs by LGBTQIA people, accounts of post-evangelical exiles, and horror stories from frustrated academics trying to enter an academy that has no good place for them. Unlike, in that this dual memoir stunningly brings these three genres together with tremendous power and pathos, and offers the most compelling and informative account of the intersex experience that I have ever seen. In the end, *Intersexion* teaches the centrality of courageous authenticity in settings where such authenticity is punished. Often, those settings are Christian. This book is a triumph.

David Gushee, Professor of Christian Ethics, author of
Changing Our Mind: The Landmark Call for Inclusion of LGBTQ Christians

Intersexion is a reminder that in a world fighting for black and white answers, authenticity is most often found in a variety of colors and hues. Danny and Cynthia's story shows that the journey toward acceptance can in one moment bring about absolute freedom and in the next crushing loss. This is not simply a memoir, but a direct challenge for all of us to live unafraid of who we truly are.

Matt Kendziera, host of the
Chasing Goodness podcast

Intersexion has so much heart and depth with Cynthia Vacca Davis weaving together two stories of courage and vision. The reader is often challenged to examine the accepted norms of identity, careers, and faith, to keep up with the protagonists' journeys. This is a good thing. These stories can inspire us to find a way forward with integrity and empathy.

Scott Okamoto, host of the
Chapel Probation podcast

The stories of intersex individuals are some of least understood and least heard in our world. Cynthia Vacca Davis's *Intersexion* is a profoundly eye opening, challenging, and ultimately inspiring exploration of the journey of an intersex individual and what it means to be a true ally to this often misunderstood and severely marginalized community. With beautiful prose and masterful storytelling, Cynthia Vacca Davis has offered us a true gift in *Intersexion*.

Rev. Brandan Robertson, author of
Dry Bones and Holy Wars: A Call for Social and Spiritual Renewal

You've never read a book like this before. I hadn't. A gripping memoir with a twist, combining two unlikely stories—of an intersex man finding himself and being found by a writer who tells his story alongside her own. Because we are going through this transformation together in hopes that, one day, everyone's story may be told and we can stop being strangers to ourselves and to each other.

Ken Wilson, pastor of Blue Ocean Church Ann Arbor and author of
A Letter to My Congregation

Intersexion

Intersexion

A Story *of*
Faith, Identity, and Authenticity

———◆———

Cynthia Vacca Davis

LAKE DRIVE
lakedrivebooks.com

Lake Drive Books
6757 Cascade Road SE, 162
Grand Rapids, MI 49546

info@lakedrivebooks.com
lakedrivebooks.com
@lakedrivebooks

Publishing books that help you heal, grow, and discover.

Softcover ISBN 978-1-957687-06-3
eBook ISBN 978-1-957687-07-0

Printed in the United States of America

Library of Congress Control Number: 2022936047

To the one in every hundred whose gender cannot be fully contained within a checkbox, and to brave people—cis, trans, straight, or gay—who are somewhere on the path to becoming their true, authentic selves

Contents

A Note from Cynthia

THE TASK OF WRITING A nonfiction narrative requires a string of decisions about what to reveal and what to conceal. "Danny," for instance, is a pseudonym. In a cultural climate where transgender and, by extension, intersex individuals are too often targeted for hate crimes, and out of respect for the new life Danny is building, changing his name was an easy choice. By extension, I was equally opaque about the exact Hampton Roads community in which Danny grew up; thus, names of schools, churches, and the people associated with those places were all changed. I opted also to protect the identities of people from my childhood—many of whom I haven't seen in decades—who perhaps would not have wanted to become literary characters.

Equally simple was the decision to withhold the name of the university at which I worked. The events that played out could have occurred at dozens, perhaps hundreds, of conservative schools in the country. In fact, during the writing of this book, I was interviewed for an article in *The Chronicle of Higher Education* about this very topic: the polarizing impact the legalization of gay marriage has had on Christian institutions. I believe spotlighting my former employer would take focus from the larger story of discrimination against both the LGBTQIA+ community and its allies, which is of infinitely more concern than doxing a single school.

On the other hand, my family and I opted to use our own names, and I chose to identify my current professional home, Christopher Newport University. It is an honor for me to be the face of this project and the keeper of the stories it contains. Additionally, I opted to share identifying details of the Azusa Pacific University story and my interactions with Adam—as he was known at the time—as they were widely covered in the news.

I used real emails, text messages, and journal entries to bolster my memories and made every effort to stay faithful to the details of how events played out. More challenging were decisions about how to portray scenes that happened as many as thirty years ago—scenes I wasn't present to witness. I drew on over a decade of experience writing human-interest stories to guide my interviews with Danny. Knowing that encounters with real people are mind-expanding tools, I worked to gather details I hoped would bring Danny to life. The scenes from Danny's childhood—informed by numerous conversations, photos, and general knowledge of the time period—represent the "movie" my mind constructed of the events, places, and people that comprised memorable moments in his life. I preserved the essence of conversations Danny related to me as faithfully as possible.

Early in the writing process, Danny and I decided to consistently use the masculine form of his name to clearly communicate his life-long self-perception and identification as male. Accordingly, the feminine form, "Dani," is used only in scenes where he is perceived from an outside point of view, and only during the time period he was presenting as female.

Danny's story is presented as it was told to me and further informed though years of living in community with Danny, for a time under the same roof. While I am not trained to speak from a medical perspective on the physiology at play in Danny's account, I can confidently attest that I was faithful to reporting Danny's story as it was told to me in tandem with my own observations. Danny's medical facts are complex, facts to which only a highly specialized medical professional could speak to after evaluating Danny, a level of analysis that is beyond the intended scope of this story or Danny's comfort.

I have my editor, Jessie Stover, to thank for another crucial story decision: the telling of Danny's story in the first person. I was reluctant to adopt Danny's "voice"—it felt too personal and invasive. Jessie dragged me kicking and screaming to the place this book ultimately landed: a dual-narrative story told in three first-person sections—and, based on beta reader reactions to the first-person Dani/Danny voice, I am grateful for her pushback to my stubbornness.

A Note from Danny

I AM SO EXCITED AND thankful that Cynthia wanted to tell my story. She has done such an excellent job of recreating my experiences as if she had been there to witness them. I hope that in bringing my story to light, others will identify with my struggles and know they're not alone. I also want to help open the eyes of those who may not be familiar with intersex or the LGBTQIA+ community, and for members of the community to know, regardless of your sexual orientation or gender identity, you are beautifully and wonderfully made just the way you are.

Prologue

Cynthia

THE LINES DISAPPEARED FROM THE asphalt as I catapulted into the pitch-black unknown. My heart thumped to the frantic flap of the windshield wipers as my knuckles went white, rigid around the steering wheel. With every brain cell focused on the six inches of pavement I could make out in front of me, I had no mental space to process that I was out this late, in this storm, because the impossible had just happened. I'd been handed a dream job—one that came with a brand-new dream life. In short, I had been right. Circuiting three universities in two states every week could lead to something. My career wouldn't cap off teaching out of a Chevy Spark with a trunkful of ungraded papers, a tumbleweed of half-clean clothes and a pile of snack wrappers riding shotgun.

A midsemester tenure-track promotion wasn't something that just happened. Especially to someone two years away from a Master of Fine Arts in creative nonfiction. It was a rare, aspirational position that had seasoned PhDs scrapping and scrambling for interviews with national search committees. It was something no adjunct instructor ever declined discussing, even after a 7:00 p.m. class at the tail end of a thirteen-hour teaching day. Even with ominous clouds looming in the weather radar report and an hour's drive ahead, there was nothing to do but stay and listen to the academic dean describe the raise, the office, the job security, the schedule tailored just for me. Maybe the storm wouldn't hit before I was past the twelve-mile stretch of unlit, unlined road. Maybe it would never come at all.

It didn't occur to me that driving blind through a storm wasn't the only threat to my brand-new life. I had no way of knowing the fast pass to the tenure track I'd just scored in the dream job lottery came at a steep cost. It would be days before I'd realize the plan I'd made with Danny the week before was tantamount to jumping the guardrails, and even if I did manage to keep my little Spark on the road, it wouldn't keep my life from derailing. Danny's story had put me on a collision course from which there was no turning back. Hearing his story had changed everything.

Danny

1
Dresses and Earrings

BEING A SIXTH GRADER WITH both a penis and a period was confusing, to say the least. But long before my momentous puberty, I was a befuddled toddler at war with a dress.

"I don't like dresses. I am a boy." I shook my tangled mop in frustration as I pulled a T-shirt and shorts from my drawer. "I want to wear *this*!"

"Danielle, you're a girl," my mother said.

"Well, I'll be a boy when I grow up!"

My parents had six children: my older brothers, Rick, Bill, and Jim; my older sisters, Barb and Mary; and me—the child they called their red-haired little girl.

Except I wasn't a girl. True, at that moment my three-year-old body looked like a girl's body, but I didn't know that. What I did know was that I seemed to be the victim of a terrible mistake. In my mind, I was clearly a boy, but everyone kept calling me a girl. How could no one see me? The other thing I was sure of was that I wanted nothing to do with the short, frilly dress my mother, Sherry, was holding.

"But the green is so pretty!" My mother sighed in exasperation. Barb and Mary loved dressing up. In fact, my mother had just recently sewn them each new dresses as a final project in a home economics class she took at the local high school. Finishing the class earned her the diploma she'd forgone twenty years earlier when she left her unstable home at sixteen to marry and move away with a young college student—my father, Ben.

I know my mother succeeded in getting me into that dress at least once, because I'm wearing it in a faded 1973 snapshot of our family outside our standard-issue house on the California air force base where we were stationed. In the photo, Dad stands on one end in a suit and tie with trim, military-regulation hair, my mother alongside him in coiffed curls and earrings. Mary, twelve, stands next to Mom, her hair long and straight. Next is Barb, the seventeen-year-old beauty queen of the family, sporting a bob and a crisp A-line dress. Then there are the shaggy heads of my brothers, Rick, nineteen, and Bill, sixteen, poking out from the back row, while Jim, nine, stands in the front. Everything about the photo—the clothing, the hair styles, the lurid red color cast—comfortably belongs in that early seventies moment. Everything except me. I stand next to Jim in a frilly green dress that barely grazes my thighs, thumb jammed in my mouth and a scowl etched on my face.

─◦◦◦─

IN MY MIND, I HAVE always been male, and I have always thought of myself in the masculine: as Dani, despite having to spell it with an *i*. Even as a toddler, I didn't understand the confusion about my gender, but I also didn't know how things worked: perhaps I had to grow into my masculinity. I was frustrated that the world saw me as a girl, but I knew who I was—I would just have to wait for everyone else to see it too. It would be decades before the word *intersex* became part of my vocabulary. These were years without facts, science, or the internet to help me understand what was happening inside my mind and, eventually, my body. Years full of question marks, fear, shame, guilt, and confusion. Years of knowing that whatever was happening to me wasn't normal and couldn't be discussed in our conservative, Christian home. Because no matter what my mind said—or what changes my body went through—I was expected to be what the world demanded: female.

My mother hoped my identification with the masculine was a passing phase. But it didn't pass. Not at our next station in Guam, where I grew into an active child with an impish smile, occasional black eye, and a tumble of tangled strawberry curls that I hated having touched or brushed. And it didn't pass in Virginia, where we moved on humanitarian orders when my mom's sister was dying of cancer and, exhausted by life events and my incessant pestering, she relented and allowed me to cut my hair—short. Very short. It was a change that ushered in the golden age of my childhood.

(

❧

DESPITE THE STRESSFUL CIRCUMSTANCES THAT brought us to Virginia, I settled into life in the close-knit military community that came complete with a self-contained elementary school. The kids in my neighborhood were a living kaleidoscope: Black, white, Asian—no one cared who you were or where you were from, as long as you were up for a lively game of tag or pickup ball. Playing outside with my friends gave me the opportunity to just be myself.

I fell in naturally with the boys in the neighborhood. I never felt detached from male camaraderie, and when it came to games of "house," the girls always assigned me the role of the dad. In fact, that's how I got my first kiss. I was hanging out with a friend one day when his sister, Maggie, came home with another girl and we all decided to play house. I was Maggie's husband. When the time came for me to go off to "work," I kissed Maggie on the lips. It wasn't sexual—it was just normal role-playing. I saw myself as a guy, and they did too. Maybe that was just wishful thinking, but that was my perception at the time.

What didn't feel normal were the types of things I felt I had to do at home to please my parents. They were constantly steering me toward feminine activities and clothing: skirts were a must at church—Sunday morning and evening. I hated every minute I spent in a skirt, and I knew how much that disappointed my mom. The guilt gnawed at me constantly. I lived for the rare moments when I felt comfortable and my parents were happy too. Like the time I was six and I somehow ended up with a *Happy Days* T-shirt. Simple things like that made me feel like myself. One evening when I was wearing it, I bounded into the living room where my parents were holding a Bible study group.

"Heyyyyy ..." I called in a deep, gravelly voice, two thumbs pointed skyward in my best Arthur Fonzarelli. The room burst into laughter. In that moment, I was the Fonz, and my parents loved it. Nothing beat the feeling of being seen and appreciated as myself, hamming it up, emulating a masculine role model. The routine became a shtick, a feel-good go-to.

In terms of emotional boosts, visits from my maternal grandmother were the anti-Fonz. She didn't enjoy kids in general. Shooing everyone outside to play was standard procedure during her stays. But my appearance and habits particularly vexed her sensibilities.

Gigi, as she was called, was an Elizabeth Taylor-esque figure in matters of both deportment and matrimony. Tall, thin, and impeccably dressed in pantsuits and jewelry, Gigi had been divorced four times before the 1960s. By the time I came along, she'd settled into permanent union with Milton, a professional musician who had earned a place in the New Orleans Jazz Museum. Milton, who went by his first name, was the sole embodiment of anything good that happened to me during our visits, whether at Milton and Gigi's house in Florida or at home in Virginia.

"Don't touch!" Gigi would say at intervals whenever the kids were in her home. "Kids need to be kids outside," was another of Gigi's mottos. "If you are going to sit inside, you're going to behave. In here, it's adult time."

Adult time was of no interest to me; I preferred to ride Milton's bike outside all day. But adult time occasionally moved outdoors when it came to waterskiing or golf, two of Gigi's pastimes. During one Florida visit, Gigi dropped my siblings and me off at Epcot Center for the day so the adults could play golf and head to the country club for dinner and dancing. My dad told me later how bitter he'd been about the whole thing; he wished Gigi had dropped him off at Epcot Center too.

When I wasn't pedaling around the neighborhood on Milton's bike or being shuttled off to an amusement park, I typically rode out our visits with Gigi in the company of Milton and Dad, watching TV and picking up guitar tips from Milton while the women shopped and lunched. Hiding out with Milton was a place of refuge, a sanctuary of sorts that came to a sudden and certain end when Gigi and Milton visited Virginia right before my tenth birthday.

Mom would always go into overdrive on these visits, putting extra effort into "fixing" me in an attempt to gain her mother's approval.

Gigi would shake her head and frown at my mother as soon as she saw me. "She is too dirty for a girl! Look at her hair! It's a mess. She's never dressed."

Mom would turn to me. "You have to act like a lady," she would say, reinforcing her expectations with a continual string of corrections: "That's not how young ladies sit," or speak, or act. But this visit was different. I was suddenly required to take part in the shopping and lunching excursions, no longer allowed to hang out around the TV with Milton and Dad.

Then came the day Mom told me to get ready to go to the mall. "Gigi is doing something special for your birthday today!"

Mom sounded thrilled, but I wasn't fooled. I knew there was no way this could be a good thing.

"We're going to take you to get your ears pierced!"

"What?" I immediately panicked. How could I get out of this? "No, please!" I was desperate and begging. "I don't want that."

"Listen," Mom said. "This is something Gigi wants to do for your birthday. You are going to do it. It means you are growing up." Her voice lightened. "You're becoming a woman!"

"That's so unfair!" Mary said when she heard the plans for the shopping trip. "The rest of us had to wait until we were sixteen to get our ears pierced! It was the rule!" But normal rules were prone to be abandoned in extreme circumstances, and it seemed that Gigi had declared my state to be one of utter emergency.

I'm sure I looked like a prisoner condemned to the gallows as I trudged through the mall. "How long do I have to keep them in?" I asked Mary.

"Just wear them when Gigi comes."

But my worries were more immediate. "I mean, how long in the beginning?"

"Six, maybe eight weeks."

My stomach sank. Dad and Jim's church softball teams were about to begin exhibition games. I waited for softball season all winter. Not only did I love to be on the softball field, but playing with the kids of the opposing teams' players gave me a chance to interact with peers who didn't know to call me "her," or that I wore skirts on Sundays and had to be reminded to act "like a young lady." Like a rancher's brand on a cow's hide, the earrings would be a mark of identity. The shiny studs would instantly label me as something I wasn't: female.

I sat in a chair in a raised booth that seemed to be in full view of the mall shoppers. I felt like a spectacle. A saleswoman showed me a display of earrings and asked me which ones I wanted. In what amounted to a last stand, I pointed at one of the men's earrings.

"Oh no," the woman said, laughing. "Those are for men. They don't come in pairs. You need to choose from these," she said, sweeping a hand across several rows of shiny studs.

I chose the tiniest cubic zirconia setting available, pinning my hopes on the possibility that the small specks could be overlooked. Resignation washed over me once the studs were through my ears. But a small bit of hope resurged as the woman explained the importance of cleaning my ears each day and underscored the risk of contamination. I silently pledged to never clean my ears and hoped that germs would accumulate into a raging infection. Much to my eventual disappointment, my ears were impervious to toxins despite my meticulous neglect. The earrings became just another thing I endured for the sake of keeping my home life as normal as possible—a challenge that would become increasingly difficult now that I'd reached my double-digit years.

Indeed, my carefree days of playing and learning within the familiar confines of the air force base were drawing to a close. Dad's retirement was approaching, and we would need to adjust to life outside the supportive structure of the Department of Defense. Even though we would be settling into a home just a few miles off base, for me the move was a permanent transition from childhood into the pressure of a larger public school—and a puberty no curriculum could have possibly prepared me for.

2

Almost Twelve

IN THE SPRING OF 1982, a small paperback book appeared beneath my door. I was by no means an avid reader, although I frequently ordered from school book-club flyers for the perks, like stickers and posters. Accordingly, my bedroom style was best characterized as late-school-year Scholastic, with images of the California Raisins, Pac-Man, and *Star Wars* plastered across my walls. But a passing glance at the slim volume on my floor—*Almost Twelve*—supported suspicions that the covert, under-the-door delivery system had already raised: this would be an uncomfortable read. I cracked the spine anyway. Maybe, just maybe, this book contained a clue, some tidbit of information that would explain the hell that had been sixth grade.

"Did you get the book?" Mom whispered later.

"Mmm hmm."

"Well, let me know if you have any questions," she said.

I knew Mom had probably breathed a prayer as the book scooted beneath the door and across the floor that there would be no questions, of any kind, ever, about the text. It wasn't a complicated request; I really had no questions— at least about the material covered in the thin paperback. Health class had covered those basics. My questions were beyond the scope of the material that Kenneth N. Taylor, of *Almost Twelve* fame, or the Virginia Department of Education seemed equipped to address.

I had already made an attempt at a real question six months earlier, when the school year was fresh and its problems were new. I was looking for the kind of answers I needed to just get through a day in my new school. Church made me a believer in miracles: Bible stories were full of healings, resurrections—time even stood still once for Joshua. But when I asked my brother Jim about the kind of miracle I needed, he could give me nothing helpful, nothing concrete to cling to as the maelstrom of sixth-grade events raged on.

❧

THE FIRST DAY OF SCHOOL began on a high. I walked into the classroom and joined three girls who'd already claimed spots near the back of the room. I slid into an open seat next to the prettiest girl, Valerie—a poster-girl cheer-leader-to-be: blonde hair and blue eyes, looks I would later see her use as currency. Kara, a petite girl with a sharp tongue and long black hair, sat on Valerie's opposite side. Jen claimed a spot one row over. I didn't see it then, but her choice of seat communicated her position in the group. She was a tagalong, a preteen with unruly brown hair who had yet to discover where she really belonged.

I had no confusion over my social status on this first day of the year. I was an outsider among cliques that had been long cemented on playground swing sets and over cartons of cool chocolate milk. Sure, it was the first day of sixth grade, but no one else was feeling uncomfortable in a new environment; I was virtually alone in that. The majority of my new classmates had been walking these halls since kindergarten.

"Nice flannel," Kara said.

Her smile signaled that it was a sincere compliment, and the other girls echoed her assessment. Flannel wasn't the obvious choice for a late-summer day in Virginia, but the shirt was brand new and I couldn't wait to wear it. Any additional warmth the shirt added now registered only as a glow to bask in.

The conversation volleyed back and forth—the girls addressing each other, and then including me. For reasons I've long forgotten—perhaps an account of a summer bike spill or dental procedure—talk turned to pain tolerance. Valerie asked for my arm.

"What? Why?" I laughed, nervous and excited.

"Like this," Valerie said, taking my arm and turning it palm up. "Have you seen this one?"

"Um … I don't think so?" I said, as Valerie began slapping my forearm. "I'm planting a garden," she said. The girls giggled as Valerie began digging her nails across the tender skin on the inside of my arm. It was then that I recognized that Valerie was performing their school's version of the painful "garden" game, a staple activity on the playground circuit. "First we need to dig the rows. Tell me when it's too much," she said, laughing, digging deeper in my skin.

"No, I'm good," I said.

Valerie increased the pressure. Her nails tugged across my skin but the pain remained tolerable. "Now we have to plant the seeds," she said, grabbing and pinching the puffed-up skin along the "rows" she'd just dug into my arm.

Valerie pulled back her hand and inspected the puffy red tracks and blotches across my skin.

"Look what I did to your arm!" she said, clapping her hand over her mouth.

"It's okay. I'm good."

"That's so cool!" Valerie was gushing in admiration.

Heck yeah, I'm good! The prettiest girl in the school just touched my arm. I think I might like this new school thing after all!

Then came lunch. The teacher, Mrs. Conway, lined everyone up in the hall at the entrance to the bathrooms.

"We're all going to wash our hands before we eat," she announced.

My heart pounded beneath the flannel that had become suddenly stifling. As a rule, I avoided public bathrooms at all costs. They were dangerous—far more dangerous than any stray germs that may or may not be on my now-sweaty palms.

I had only met Mrs. Conway one other time, but I had not been assigned to her class by random selection. Mom had chosen Mrs. Conway—an old friend who'd been in her wedding—as my teacher to "keep an eye" on me, the "daughter" she was increasingly worried about.

From my place in line, it seemed clear that the day—the entire year, in fact—was taking a sharp turn, but I dug in my heels.

"My hands aren't dirty!" I stood in place, shaking my head.

"Everyone needs to go, Dani."

"But—"

"Go on," Mrs. Conway said.

My legs were heavy. The few yards to the door seemed like miles. I could feel my face flush even hotter and I felt woozy and faint as I approached the door I was expected to open.

Then it happened.

"That boy is going into the girls' room! Stop him!" It was Jerry Binker, a bully who would, from this moment forward, make it his personal mission to make sixth grade my own personal *Inferno*.

"No," Mrs. Conway jumped in. "That's Danielle. She's a girl."

There it was. The flannel shirt; the scratched arm, puffy with red badges of masculinity; the giggling admiration of the popular girls: none of it mattered now. I was done. Labeled. A freak. The looks of jaw-dropping shock followed by the anger that flashed across Valerie, Kara, and Jen's faces said more than words ever could.

～・～

A FEW WEEKS INTO THE school year I was lying in bed, trying to quiet my thoughts enough to get to sleep. My guinea pig, Patches—a creature with far fewer worries—had settled down into the wood shavings that lined his cage and gave the room a light cedar aroma.

Why do things have to be this way? How is God going to work this out for me? Is he ever going to change me into a boy? Really, truly, fully, in a way that everyone can see?

I continued to toss and turn until my eyes settled on my shelf of rabbit figurines. Mom would find these figures of bunnies wearing sunglasses or swinging a baseball bat—fun, but nothing too girly—and give them to me as gifts. I liked them a lot; they were a way Mom found to connect with me. I loved my mother, but I knew I couldn't talk with her about the stuff that kept me awake. I knew, instinctually, that the worries of my inner life were taboo. By this time, it was just Mary, Jim, and me living at home. I could hear Jim in the bathroom across the hall. My brother was eighteen now and really popular with girls. I wanted everything he had, especially his wardrobe. I often raided his dresser, liberally borrowing his jeans and T-shirts. I decided to put some feelers out to see if Jim could help.

I heard the doorknob turn as Jim left the bathroom. "Jim? Can you come here for a minute?"

He came in the room and stood at the foot of the bed, next to Patches's cage.

I sat up. "If you are, say, a guinea pig and there's, um," my eyes darted across the room, settling on the shelf of figurines, "rabbits that you are hanging out with and you are trying to help them, will God change you into a rabbit?"

Spiritual metaphor seemed the best path into the topic. And if Jim seemed confident that God could change one species into another to support God's purpose, then clarifying a gender would be no problem.

"No, Dani," Jim said. "It doesn't work that way. God would either find a way to use the guinea pig, or he'd find another rabbit."

This was not the response I was hoping to hear. I wanted my brother to say that of *course* God would make that guinea pig into a rabbit. God could do anything, right?

I continued to pray. And then, miraculous, joyous changes began to take place. Actual, visual changes. Something between my legs began to get larger, and longer, and a single sphere descended from wherever it had been hiding deep inside my body. Jim, apparently, was wrong. God was turning me into a rabbit.

ε∾∾ə

"MARY, I'M BLEEDING!"

I'd just returned from a softball game and, as usual, ran straight for the bathroom. I could spend an entire day on the ball field and never use the restroom. Avoiding public bathrooms was even higher on my personal list of priorities than dodging a tag-out at home plate.

When I pulled down my white baseball pants, I was alarmed to see a bright red stain in the crotch—fresh blood.

My mind raced with possibilities. Groin injury? Could something be torn or ripped? I tried to remember anything significant that happened on the field that day. Had I been hit with a pitch? Any daring slide-ins to bases? Could it be a kidney? Cancer? Oh, no. *Could it be cancer?* My thoughts flashed back to leaving Guam and moving in with my grandparents so my mom could care for my aunt Rachael who had cancer and *died*.

My thoughts raced, my face burned, and my stomach roiled. I wasn't sure what was worse: death, or having to go to the doctor. Because next to praying for a body that would match my insides, I prayed for good health—no high fevers, no rashes, and certainly no internal bleeding—nothing that would prompt a visit to a doctor's office. The last thing I needed was someone examining my body, asking questions.

Mary came to the bathroom door, and I showed her the stain on my pants. "Don't worry about it." She seemed completely unfazed. "It's your period."

"My what?" I was panicked and screaming.

"Just go look under the sink."

"No, it can't be that. There's just no way."

"Dani, it's normal. Get something from under the sink." Mary was annoyed.

I stumbled back into the bathroom, numbed by the news. I looked under the sink and found a package of *things*, girl products, stuff I didn't know anything about and had no desire to learn. I knew from health class and Kenneth N. Taylor that periods existed and were for girls, but I tuned out after that. My hands shook as I fumbled with the box. I remembered nothing from health. I was forced to attend the girl class and I mentally checked out during the talk about periods and the ghastly birthing videos—anything involving blood. I hated blood. The topic didn't involve me, anyway; I was a boy. I was sure of it back in class, and then it became clear. God was turning me into a rabbit ... wasn't he?

My mind raced. *No, no, it cannot be that. This isn't supposed to happen. How can I have both? Everything was moving in a really good way, and now I have both? I don't want both! I'm a guinea pig with rabbit ears!*

AT SCHOOL, THE MEAN GIRLS ruled my world. The *Almost Twelve* episode with Mom confirmed that sex organs were not a topic of household conversation, but that didn't mean I was completely without support.

My mom knew I was having a tough year and offered encouragement in the form of daily notes in my lunch bag. Some days the notes featured a Bible verse, other times, an "I love you" or good wishes that I would find a new friend. I kept these notes in an old brown lunch bag in the back of my desk to cheer me up on bad days. Days like the ones when Binker would wait until most of the class was within earshot then point at my shoes and scream "butter cookies," sixth-grade slang for off-brand tennis shoes. White canvas Nikes with a baby-blue swoosh were a status symbol; wearing butter cookies implied that you were too poor for the good shoes. I spent most of the year kicking around in lookalikes Mom bought at the base before she realized the problem and finally bought me some Nikes.

One day I walked into the classroom and saw Binker at my desk, pulling a white paper from a crumpled brown bag.

"Okay, guys, here's one: "'For I know the plans I have for you,' declares the Lord. 'Plans to prosper you and not to harm you. Plans to give you hope and a future.'" God has big plans for you, Dani. Love, Mom."

The class howled. Kara perched on a desk near Binker. "Come on, hurry, read the next one," she coaxed.

I slid into my seat and blinked back tears.

"What's going on here?" Mrs. Conway demanded as she entered the room.

Binker snickered. "Just like always, Dani, your best friend, Mrs. Conway, saved the day."

◦⸱⸱◦

SIXTH GRADE FINALLY ENDED, AND it was summer. I was beginning to adjust to my new body. Although I wasn't a fan of my current situation, I knew I'd figure something out. I continued to pray that God would make me fully male. After all, if new parts could appear, old ones could go away. Anything was possible.

Including one more surprise my body had in store. Sometime that summer, my nipples began to hurt and seemed to swell. Then the area around my nipples got larger too. As if a penis, a testicle, and a bleeding vagina weren't enough for a pubescent preteen to handle, it became impossible to ignore the fact that I now had breasts too.

3
Labels

HAVING BREASTS MADE IT MORE difficult to pass as male, but I was determined to figure something out. So, late that summer, I began sneaking T-shirts from Jim's drawer on a daily basis. I took the shirts to my room and began experimenting in front of my bedroom mirror, eventually landing on a multi-step, self-designed chest-binding system. My initial efforts involved a shirt and two belts, but I eventually added a second shirt to the configuration. After several dry runs, I had the process streamlined in time for the first day of seventh grade.

When I got up that morning, I pulled a pilfered T-shirt over my head and cinched it tightly under one of the belts. Then I reached behind my back and yanked on the shirttail, hiking the collar up to my neck in front. Next, I pulled the shirt taut beneath my belt buckle and wrapped the excess fabric around the leather strap. Once my foundation was secure, I slid into one of my signature long-sleeved, button-up flannel shirts and tucked it into my jeans. I looped a second belt around the outside to secure everything and surveyed the results in the mirror.

I was optimistic about the new school year. Although the hallways were peopled with familiar faces—Binker, Valerie, Kara, and Jen—this was junior high: a new, big building filled with students who came from several different schools. In my mind, that represented hope. And it took only until second-period health class to realize my optimism was not completely misplaced.

Health and PE classes were scheduled on alternating days, and both were held in the gym. Students chose their own seats on the bleachers and clumped in predictable formations. Outliers like me sat alone on the periphery. I was okay with that; being by myself was preferable to being taunted.

"Hi. I'm Abby." The voice jolted me out of my thoughts. I looked up and saw a waif-thin girl with long brown hair wearing a mishmash of stripes and plaids and clutching a sketchbook and a copy of *The Exorcist*. Abby may just as well have been walking around in a sandwich board proclaiming herself a nonconformist.

Abby slid across the bleachers and took a seat beside me. "What school did you come from?" she asked.

We swapped the names of our elementary schools. I knew a couple of people from my youth group who had gone to her school. I rattled off the names of everyone on the it-group roster, but none of them sounded familiar to Abby.

"What do you like to do?" I asked.

"I read," Abby said, laughing, raising *The Exorcist* with one hand, "and draw," she added, lifting her sketchbook with the other hand. "You?"

"Softball," I said, lobbing an invisible pitch toward the gym floor.

Abby and I compared schedules and discovered that we had all the same classes. We instantly became two friends in an eventual threesome that included Abby's boyfriend, Paul. Stick thin with straight, flat hair, Paul was ahead of his time: emo before the term was coined.

We began to share a table at lunch, where conversation often turned to speculating about how we collectively became misfits.

"They call me a freak," was all I could manage about my circumstances.

Paul was more specific. "I'm attracted to guys," he whispered across the lunch table one day.

I shot a look in Abby's direction.

"She knows," Paul said. "It's something I'm working on."

I asked Abby about it one day when we were alone. "You really okay with Paul liking guys?" I asked.

"He just needs love," Abby said.

"It just kind of seems like maybe he's not into this as much as you are," I said.

"No, he loves me," Abby said. "He'll come around. In the meantime, it gives him something to tell the bullies."

Paul, numbered among Binker's victims, was teased mercilessly for his delicate mannerisms and speech patterns. Abby and I didn't share any classes with Binker, but Paul wasn't as fortunate. The two classes he didn't have with Abby and me were with Binker. By virtue of proximity, Binker's primary target shifted from me to Paul.

Securing a place where I belonged—even if it was with misfits—gave me courage in more challenging second-period circumstances. PE had always been my favorite class, but it had been so much easier in elementary school when it was just fun and games, before the curveball that was the junior high locker room and its forced communal showers.

The locker room smelled of sweat, soap, and stick deodorant that the girls slathered liberally over their breasts and backs. Talk was mostly about bodies; notes were compared, experiences shared.

"It happened on vacation, wearing a brand-new pair of shorts," one girl whined. "We were at a restaurant and my sister whispered to me to go with her to the bathroom. I had a huge red stain. It was so *embarrassing* and my shorts were ruined."

"I was so scared," said another girl. "And my stomach hurt. I didn't think it would be like that."

I remembered how scared I was when my period came. I began wondering if my experience was like anyone else's. As the girls would talk about their periods, growing breasts, and bras, I scanned the conversation for key words, clues, any hint that someone else had a body that was changing in ways similar to mine.

Abby never participated in these conversations. Her locker was tucked in an inconspicuous alcove in the back of the room, and she typically did her business and went on her way, unnoticed. For me, the locker room represented the possibility that life could somehow make sense. I scanned the locker-room chatter for any scrap of useful information, any potential key that could explain my existence. I was a listener, a lurker, never an active participant in the conversation. But, over time, I began to feel like I was somehow part of the group. The situation seemed communal and intimate. Valerie and Kara were even there, talking freely about their bodies in front of me. Things were better now, I told myself. Things were normal. Everyone was going through a lot of crazy changes—not just me. And maybe it was okay to talk about it.

One day the subject was pubic hair: who had it, what it looked like, how it felt, where it was growing. Fresh from the shower, several girls hitched up their towels to show each other the coarse, alien patches of growth sprouting across their private areas.

Now's the time. Test the waters. I summoned my courage. "So, um, is it normal for someone to have, um, other things going on down there?"

"Other things? Like what?" someone asked.

"Um, like, you know, other things than what we've discussed." I shrugged, trying to be casual.

Eyes darted around the room; brows furrowed. "Like sweating?" someone offered.

"No, no, nothing like that." My face burned.

"Do you mean, like, pain?" someone else tried.

I shook my head.

"Itching?" someone suggested.

"No, no," I said, squeezing my eyes shut and taking a deep breath. "Like you've got, you know, both guy and girl parts."

The room went silent for a moment. Zippers stopped short. Brushes halted mid-stroke. When the response came, it was collective, vehement, and final. "*Eww!*"

"That's freaky." Valerie said, pulling her brush through her long, wet hair. "That's not normal."

***

"WHAT'S GOING ON?" PAUL ASKED that afternoon as we were waiting in the hallway for our parents to pick us up after school. I kept to myself all afternoon, my insides twisted in anger, confusion, and embarrassment.

"I don't really want to talk about it. Something bad happened earlier today in the locker room."

"Why do you care so much what they think?" Abby said, a large, bright-pink flower bobbing up and down as she spoke. "They are so mean to you."

THE NEXT PE DAY, I added a new item of clothing to my daily ensemble: a gym shirt, layered between my flannel and the two binding T-shirts. I was quickly becoming a walking wardrobe. I stuffed my athletic shorts into my book bag. I had a plan to eliminate the before-class locker-room trip. A covert stop at an empty restroom at the tail end of first period allowed me to ditch my outer layer of clothing, pull on my shorts, and slide into the gym without incident.

It was the time after PE that became the bigger problem. Multiple T-shirts, thick flannel, puberty, and physical activity caused me to sweat profusely.

I became adept at averting my gaze and refusing to make eye contact with anyone; anything to keep the girls from making a scene about me being in the room with them. I tried sharing a locker with Abby, in hopes that I could adopt her inconspicuous locker-room routine, but it was too late for me to become invisible: I was labeled.

"Is the freak going to take a shower?" Valerie stage-whispered as I walked through the locker-room door.

Nervous laughter rippled through the room.

"I'm serious," Valerie said. "I'm really uncomfortable." She turned to me. "Please don't watch me." Her eyes were pleading and her tone bordered on hysteria.

It was ridiculous—all for show. I'd never been naked in the locker room before, and I certainly wasn't going to start now. But I was done being in that room.

At the end of the next PE class, I tuned to Abby. "I know I stink. I can't go in there. I can't be made fun of."

"It's okay," she said. "They pick on me too. Screw them."

"Will you guys help me?"

"Of course."

When class was over, I began lingering. I would duck under the bleachers or into a corner where I would wait for Paul to give a signal when he thought all the girls had filed out of the locker room. Abby would then go into the room and do a physical check to make sure it was empty. Only then would I slip in, change as quickly as possible, and attempt to get to class before racking up another in a growing pile of tardy slips.

MOM CAME INTO MY ROOM one evening and sat down on the edge of the bed. "I know what you're doing," she said, softly. "Why are you trying to hide who you are?" Her voice shook with emotion. "What you're doing to your body, tying it down like that, isn't healthy."

I didn't know how to respond. I was terrified of disappointing my parents, and it made me sick to think that I had caused Mom pain and worry. I mumbled some unconvincing reassurances—careful to neither lie nor tell the truth. Long after Mom said goodnight and shut my bedroom door, I lay awake with the knowledge that there was no way to win.

The only thing I wanted was to make my parents proud. But how could I do that and still be myself? My answer so far had been to separate my school life from my church and home lives. At school I had a shot at being something close to my real self—thus the binding—but at home and church I never had a chance. At home, I lived in fear of disappointing my family. At church, well…as far back as I could remember, something seemed a little off at church. Feminine behavior wasn't just preferred; it was enforced. I was still expected to wear a skirt to church both Sunday morning and evening. My mother's friends still viewed me as "Sherry's redheaded baby girl."

I'd managed to scrape by relying on a secret superpower. I discovered that the adults prized something even more than physical appearance: knowledge. Parents—even my own—would forgive a few grooming missteps if I knew the most verses, said the most prayers, and won the most Bible quiz games. At church, being the most spiritual was the fast pass to popularity.

Being popular at church made my parents proud. It was my coping mechanism, and, so far, it had served me well. At least until Mom was in my bedroom on the verge of tears over the way I was presenting my body.

And recently my church image had fallen into question too, following a conversation with my friend Megan that continued to haunt me. Megan and her sister, Tess, were the senior pastor's daughters, and they were about the best friends I had. In my mind, Tess was one of the guys; we played outside when the weather was good and watched sports on TV when it wasn't. Megan, on the other hand, was a girly girl, pretty and popular like Valerie and her friends, except she had always treated me with a gentleness and kindness I'd never felt before.

I hadn't really expected to have to give account for the disparity between my school and church personas. Sure, I had invited Abby and Paul to come with me to church events a few times, but if they'd noticed that church me was different from school me, they hadn't said anything. Then one of mean-girl Kara's friends started coming to youth group. She hit it off with Megan and they began talking. I hadn't even known this person at school, but she certainly knew who I was.

"Dani's completely different here than she is at school," she told Megan. "The way she dresses, the kind of friends she hangs out with—it's like she's not even the same person. Something's fake."

Megan asked me what was going on. "The school Dani that I heard about isn't someone I know. It's like you are living a double life." The words stung, especially coming from Megan. Sweet, kind Megan suggested I might be a fraud.

I never expected to have to account for the differences between my school and church personas, so I had no idea what to say. As much as it scared me to admit it, I realized that maybe she was right. Maybe I was a fake. I didn't know what I was, really. Male on the inside, sure, but the outside—the part that really seemed to matter—was less straightforward.

The locker-room experience was enough to convince me that my body wasn't following any sort of normal plan. I saw enough during those changing sessions to be confident that I wasn't physically female. But as much as it hurt to admit, I wasn't male, either. What was I, then? What was left? Could Valerie have been right? Was I a freak? Some sort of one-of-a-kind mishmash of body parts? The questions hammered through my head without answers, though I stared into the darkness for what felt like hours every night attempting to find some.

In the end, it was Valerie who supplied the first word I had for myself. It happened one day in the hall outside the gym. She caught my eyes and stared straight at me.

"There's the hermaphrodite." She spat the word from her lips like it was an accidental swig of sour milk—foul, offensive, objectionable. I didn't need to look the word up to know that it was a synonym for "outcast," but as soon as I was home from school, I headed straight for the large bookshelf in the living room and homed in on the encyclopedias, pulling the *H* volume from the shelf.

I hadn't yet seen any of the monstrous imagery of hermaphrodites in old texts and paintings, but as I opened the book, I instinctively braced myself to see something horrific and grisly. They called me a freak, after all. I steeled myself as I flipped through the pages. But when I found the right page and read the clinically worded definition describing a person with male and female body parts, I felt something like relief. Now I knew. I had been certain that something was different about me, and now I knew what to call it.

The information wasn't useful in terms of direction or hope, but it supplied me with a name, a label that would stick in my mind for the next thirty years.

4
Faking It

"SOME OF YOU HERE TONIGHT are just faking it," the sensei said.

It had only been a few weeks since Mom and Megan separately and simultaneously suggested I might be a fake, so the man on the stage had my full attention. We were at an event called Karate for Christ. Since my father was also my youth group leader, programs like these were a staple of my growing-up years, and they all followed a predictable format. There would be a headlining event with a "cool" factor—in this case breaking boards, high kicks, and targeted punches—that would entertain and prime the crowd. At the apex of excitement, the tone would take a radical shift toward the serious. Dead serious. One minute we'd be in the throes of cheers and laughter, the next, we'd be pondering the eternal fate of our souls should we happen to be hit by a bus on the way home. It was always buses: you'd think public transportation was flattening people on a daily basis for the number of times I'd considered this particular fate. We'd pause in contemplation, and then there would be tears, the "sinner's prayer," and soft music. The "good news" and the "plan of salvation" would be laid out. It was a familiar script and a familiar message, at least in my head. I knew I was supposed to believe that Christ died for my sins and rose from the grave. I was good with that. A lifetime of honing my super-Christian superpower meant knowing all the right answers. But what was real? How much was I faking?

I knew the truth in Megan's accusation that I was fake. My circle of seventh-grade school friends expanded as I cultivated an androgynous image that seemed to draw me into a different crowd. In 1983 androgyny was trending, and I embraced that fact like a lifeline. Presenting an ambiguous image was comforting to me. I felt relief when people were confused about my gender. In my mind, if people were confused, it meant passing as male was still an option. And that was an option I wanted to keep open as long as I possibly could.

"Just faking it." The sensei's words ran through my head as I saw myself through Megan's perspective. Scripture-quoting, prayer-leading Dani didn't mesh with the report that came to her from school: "Dani looks different. Dani talks different. Dani acts different." I didn't like causing that kind of confusion. I hadn't spent much time thinking about Megan's reaction; I never thought I would need to. I never considered the possibility that my disparate lives would intersect and that I'd have to account for the inconsistency.

Double life. Megan's words echoed in my brain as the sensei continued to speak.

What version of me was true? I was good at doing church, but my behaviors there were robotic—certainly not genuine. I felt more authentic at school, but that person made my mom cry.

The sensei was talking about getting real, about how God didn't care who you were or what you'd done—he loved you.

I hate who I am. I don't even know what I am.

"God loves you," the sensei repeated. "He really, really loves you."

The idea that God could actually love me—despite everything—hit me for the first time. I'd heard the words all my life, but for some reason in that moment I saw God as the only one who knew the real me, inside and out. He knew home me, church me, and school me and still loved me. The thought that God could see me in all those contexts and still love me made my faith feel real for the first time that night. It became about more than a bunch of verses and facts, more than a building that was just another venue to navigate. It became something tangible, and I knew that meant making an effort to reconcile who I was with what I'd been faking.

⧡

I MET SAM, THE RINGLEADER of my new friend group, during art class. Olive-skinned, muscular, and a head taller than most of the other students, Sam wore her dark hair cropped close against her scalp. She seemed drawn to my tomboy persona as I gravitated to oversized, heavily patterned shirts intended to draw eyes away from my chest. Sam liked my tough front and began to introduce me to her world and friends.

Sam's best friend was Lisa Mason, who wore her wavy, blonde hair long and her jeans skin tight. She tended toward tied halter tops, a sharp tongue, and risky recreation. She peddled marijuana and speed but left the harder stuff to her older brother, Ron. Lisa was Ron's protégé, and Sam was Lisa's bodyguard. The Masons were infamous for their parent-sponsored parties, complete with a full buffet of illegal substances. I would never have been allowed to go to any of these parties, and I never asked. I wasn't interested in the drug scene, but it was kind of nice to have a couple of popular friends—even friends who I knew to be the wrong kind of popular. Even better: it was nice to have friends who encouraged my attempts at masculinity.

I wanted to be a good Christian, and I knew part of that involved figuring out how to make my parents happy without being completely miserable. It was impossible for me not to notice how happy Mom was whenever I did something feminine. I knew that the quickest way to make Mom proud and to prove I was serious about my faith was to explore my female side. The idea was completely foreign. It went against every instinct I had, but it was what my parents and church wanted, so it had to be the right thing to do. Maybe if I gave it an honest try, I could warm up to it—maybe even become happy somehow. I had no idea how to go about such a transformation. But then I realized that Joe, a boy from science class, had been asking me a question that might provide a good place to start.

Joe was a blond-haired, sporty guy—in more of a recreational than JV superstar kind of way. I had class with him the last two periods each day. We struck up a friendship that revolved around discussions about video games and, occasionally, whether I would go out with him. In seventh grade, "going out" was more of a title than an event, but it was a title that could go a long way toward helping me fit in with the girls—which would make my parents happy and, by extension, make me a better believer.

So the next time Joe asked me out, I said yes. We still talked about sports and video games, but now we also held hands as we walked together to science, our final class of the day. I hated it. It was disgusting and I felt miserable inside, but I kept it up for two full weeks. The title, the handholding, the internal misery—it was all for a greater cause. Until one day when we were leaving class and heading toward the bank of lockers just outside the classroom door. I was miserable. And it showed.

"What's up with you today?" Joe asked.

"Nothing."

"What?" Joe prodded, "Is it your time of the month?"

In an instant, Joe was against the lockers. My right hook exploded across his nose. Blood splattered through the air; cheers erupted from the crowd of onlookers clustering around the action. I simply walked out the door and toward home, a teen boy masquerading as a tough, newly single girl.

5

Megan

IT WAS TO BE SHORT-LIVED singlehood. Not long after I sent Joe into the lockers I found myself in a new relationship. It hadn't been the plan, but I learned through youth group chatter that Tommy, a guy I played video games with after church softball, was interested in being my boyfriend. I wasn't broadsided, then, when I received a hand-scrawled note from Tommy, crafted in the classic will-you-go-out-with-me-check-yes-or-no style. Since being Tommy's girlfriend seemed to require nothing beyond continuing to play video games at each other's houses after church softball games, I checked the box next to the word *yes*.

Although it may seem as if I was following the same logic that had resulted weeks earlier in blood-spattered lockers, this time my motives strayed from the spiritual into something far more self-serving and way more interesting. Tommy was a harmless cover—something to divert attention and head off suspicion so I could pursue my true interest: Megan, the pastor's daughter. She was not just my best friend; she was the one who consumed my thoughts and elevated my heart rate. Whenever I heard Steve Miller crooning "Abracadabra" on the radio, it was Megan's big, brown eyes and voluminous, dark-blonde hair that popped into my head. I was so focused on Megan and our potential relationship that I even attempted to explain myself to her. It was terrifying but also necessary, because the feelings weren't one-sided— and Megan was worried and confused.

The prior summer, Megan, Tess, and I had been hanging out at the girls' house. Megan and I began goofing around, pretending we were married—a preteen version of the childhood game of house that led to my first kiss with Maggie on the air force base years earlier. Tess joked that if Megan and I were married, we were going to have to kiss. So we did—a few simple, sweet brushes of our lips that replayed in my memory every night when I went to bed and every morning when I woke.

The kiss must have stayed with Megan, too, because she was tormented. She was certain that she liked boys but confused by the pull she felt toward me. I scared her, and I knew I had to try to explain what was happening.

As we were walking around the front yard of the church building while our parents were in Wednesday-evening choir practice, I began sweating. "God is changing me," I said.

"What do you mean, changing you?" Megan asked.

"He's changing me into a boy. It's already happening. I promise you."

"How can that be?" Megan demanded.

"I don't know." I knew I sounded ridiculous. I was banking on our trust, our friendship, hoping it was enough for her to buy into a story that seemed to defy logic. But I owed her the truth. I took a deep breath. "I'm a boy, but no one understands yet. So, I'm praying that God will change me in ways that everyone will see, and it's already starting to work."

"How do you know?" she asked.

"I'm changing," I said. "My body is changing. Soon everyone will see."

"But how can that be? I don't notice anything different. I don't understand." Megan was calm, but skeptical.

"I know it's hard. But God does miracles, right? We talk about that all the time in church: God parting the Red Sea for the Israelites, people getting healed and raised from the dead—all kinds of things. God doesn't change—he can still do miracles."

"But I have never heard of him changing anyone from a girl to a boy. Why would he do that?" My heart sank. She wasn't buying it.

"He already is! And it's going to keep happening, I know it."

I knew that staying on the spiritual track was the best chance I had to convince her. That gave me an idea. We both knew the Old Testament story of Gideon: how God told him to attack the Midianites, but he wasn't sure it was really God. As a test to see if the message was truly divine, he set a fleece of sheep's wool outside his tent and prayed that God would make the fleece wet in the morning but leave the ground dry. The next morning, Gideon wrung a wet fleece out onto dry ground. But he wanted one more sign, and so he asked that the reverse would be true the next morning: wet ground and dry fleece. The next day dawned with soaking grass and bone-dry fleece. Gideon's story was popular in church circles, and adults often used it as a model for spiritual decision-making. "Putting out a fleece" was common practice—a tool to eliminate ambiguity. Not sure what to do? Spell out the sign you want to see. Ask God to clarify.

"How about we put out a fleece?" I said. "If God is really changing me, if I am really becoming male, let's ask him to show you."

"Okay, what do we pray for?" Megan asked, excited by the possibility of bearing witness to a miracle.

"Well, you know how I am really regular with, uh, that time of the month?" I blushed. "How about we pray that if God is really changing me, he will make it go away for, say, two months." I settled on a figure that seemed remotely plausible, but not at all probable, considering that I hadn't missed a single cycle since that fateful afternoon on the softball field. "Not late or anything," I clarified, "just two months in a row, missed completely."

"Okay," Megan said. "I will pray that with you. We'll see what happens."

I cannot claim to have set up this test in complete confidence. I was frustrated by how long it was taking for God to answer my prayers. I fully expected to wake up one day to find that everyone understood, that they suddenly saw me as myself, for who I was, who I'd always been. It seemed God was interested in my case; what had happened to my body already was miraculous. But how long was it going to take to become fully effective? When would others be able to see changes? The fleece prayer was important, not just to prove to Megan that I really was changing, but as a boost to my own faith too.

While it seemed unclear which direction my miracle would take, things at school were following a more predictable path. I was still hanging around the edges of the fast crowd, but it was getting harder to avoid getting pulled into their destructive orbit. Sam and Lisa were becoming more daring with their drug use, as I discovered firsthand one day during PE.

It was a free day—a largely unsupervised free-for-all during which students enjoyed full access to equipment, balls, and the gym floor while the coach hid in his office, emerging at infrequent intervals to make sure a quorum of students were still accounted for. I usually spent free days on the bleachers with Abby and Paul, but this time I ventured into a corner where Sam, Lisa, and several of their friends were rifling through a lunch box.

"Brownies!" I said, reaching for a dark brown square as I approached the group.

"Ummm ... I wouldn't eat those," someone cautioned.

"Why not? It's *chocolate*," I said, taking a big bite, "my favorite!"

Soon I was feeling amped and overly energetic. I enjoyed the sensation at first, but it wasn't long before I was running around the gym, shooting hoops and sweating profusely.

Sam and Lisa were laughing as they watched me ping from one thing to the next. Their laughter infuriated me. I tried to stop running, stop sweating, stop moving, but I was no longer in control. It was awful. I kind of burned out energy-wise after class and went on autopilot—just sailing through a day I couldn't remember afterward. I found out later that the brownies were laced with speed, a staple among the Mason siblings' crowd.

Although that particular brownie distribution went unnoticed, Lisa and Sam's luck was about to run out. A few days later I stayed home sick from school, and when I returned, neither of the girls was there. I relied on gossip and tidbits to fill in the story. Lisa and Sam had been taking drugs in the bathroom when a teacher came in. Lisa, standing by a sink, tossed a small package to Sam, who tossed the package into the toilet and flushed. Both girls were suspended. Lisa eventually returned to school, but Sam, who was caught in the act of flushing the drugs, never did.

Although my parents never found out about the brownies or my friends' suspension, by the time spring came, they were hearing enough other news to cause them to question my future in the public school system. One afternoon, I came home and found Mom in front of the TV.

"Did you know this was happening?" she asked, pointing toward the screen where a local news anchor was reporting live from my school. According to the report, a student brandished a knife on campus during an altercation over the alleged rape of a white student by her black ex-boyfriend.

I paused for a moment to listen. "Yeah, I knew about this," I said, confused. The report was portraying the situation as a race issue: a Black-on-white crime, but everyone at school knew the girl was lying. She'd admitted that much.

I opened my mouth to try to explain, but Mom was caught up in the furor. "Did you see it happen?" she demanded.

"No, Mom, I didn't see it. I wasn't there."

"You never felt in danger?"

"No!" I said, "I heard about it after it was over. It's okay. I'm okay."

Another day, I asked my parents a question about a homework assignment for an in-class debate and unknowingly confirmed my parents' suspicions that my school situation needed to change.

I tapped my pencil on the kitchen table. "I am trying to decide who to put on this lifeboat," I said. I've got nine spots but fifteen people drowning."

"What is this assignment for?" Dad asked.

"It's a debate. We're imagining a ship has gone down and we have to decide who to save."

"Oh, I know the exercise," Dad said. "But this is not something that's an appropriate conversation for junior high," he boomed. "Deciding who to get rid of? We shouldn't even be talking about such a thing."

"All life is sacred, Dani. Only God can judge," Mom said.

My parents' concerns about the lifeboat debate were strong enough to warrant a meeting with the principal. Despite the principal's sympathy with their argument, which led to the cancelation of the in-class debate, Mom and Dad began to research private school options for me.

After tagging along with my parents on visits to a couple of small Christian schools and a large Catholic high school, I was braced for change. My parents sat me down in the living room one late-summer day. I was expecting to hear that I wouldn't be returning to school with Abby, Paul, Lisa, Valerie, Kara, Binker, and all the other personalities that had, in many ways, shaped my self-image over the previous months and years. What I wasn't prepared for was their decision about *how* things were going to change.

"Dani," Mom said, as I settled into the sofa, "your father and I have decided that homeschooling is the best option for our family."

"Homeschooling?" I was incredulous. "What about Calvary Christian or St. Mary's?"

"Dani," Dad said, "this is what's best right now. Those private schools are expensive."

"This is a great opportunity for you to do well," Mom said. "Why not give it a try? Just for the year. In ninth grade, you can go to public high school with your friends. We just need to get you out of this situation right now."

I nodded in acceptance. I wanted what was best for the family, and it was just for a year. "Sure," I said. "I'll give it a try."

"It's just for a year. Just until high school."

It didn't take long for me to start seeing the benefits of home education. For starters, I didn't have to get up and actually go anywhere. Even though I phased out binding at the end of seventh grade, erasing the entire dressing-for-school dilemma was a relief. And I loved being able to hyper-focus on a single subject until I mastered it. I was using a go-at-your-own-pace curriculum that was shipped to us from a satellite school, and it made me feel successful at school for the first time.

My days quickly fell into a predictable pattern. For the first month, our mornings began with a ringing phone.

"Would you get that, Dani?" Mom would call. "It's what's-her-face from the office."

Every single morning at the same time I'd lift the phone receiver and hear the school secretary's voice. "You are supposed to be in class."

"Um, no, I'm not."

"No, you are."

"I'm homeschooled now."

"Let me talk to your mother."

The call became a routine that gave Mom and me a laugh each morning. It also became a school bell—a signal that it was time to get to work so I could be finished before my friends got home in the afternoon. At first I tried to keep up with Abby and Paul, but our friendship began to fade. My parents encouraged me to invite my church friends over, opening the possibility of spending even more time with Megan.

Megan was my world. I was eager for her to believe that I was changing. After we prayed, I missed exactly two cycles. Then my prior schedule of clockwork periods resumed. I clung to that miraculous two-month hiatus; it was my assurance that God hadn't forgotten me. It let me know that God was still working, my body was still changing, and one day, one joyous day, everyone would see. The missed periods had also heightened Megan's belief that maybe—just maybe—my hopes weren't unfounded, that transformation might yet be possible.

"If you do become a guy, I want to be your girlfriend," Megan said time and again, whenever I reminded her that God was changing me. "Until then, we are best friends." It was enough for now. It had to be. Plus, the arrangement came with an added perk in that it saved me from uncomfortable social situations, particularly the kind that were common at Christian Skate Night.

These evenings were a big deal for Christian teens. Church youth groups from all over the community would come together and rent out the roller rink. For several hours, the venue was ours—our people, our music. Teens came from everywhere. For me, new people always represented a chance to be perceived as male—and that frequently happened. As exciting as it was when girls would flirt with me, the attention presented a dilemma when they approached me during couples' skates. If I accepted their advances, I risked raised eyebrows from my youth group and, worse, Dad. Why was I skating with a random girl? On the other hand, if I refused their advances, I risked hurt feelings or, worse, blowing my masculine persona. My bond with Megan opened another option. Now, the second the rink lights dimmed, I'd scan the room. If I saw any girls heading in my direction, I'd lock eyes with Megan.

Help. I'd mouth the single word, and she'd smoothly skate toward me and grab my hand, an action that my admirers would see as a sign that I was taken and my friends and father would see as two close girlfriends enjoying some fun. While I occasionally regretted not being able to skate with another girl to conjure some jealousy in Megan, those feelings were fleeting. I was skating with Megan!

As the year wore on, I began to get excited about my prospects for high school. The lease on our house was coming to an end, and my family began looking for a new home. One of the top contenders was in an absolute dream location—a block away from Megan. Megan! The person who understood me. The one who knew I would someday be a boy and would be waiting for me when it happened.

"It has a horseshoe driveway," I said, describing the house to her over the phone one afternoon. "And Mom really seemed to like it—she used words like *cute* and *charming*, so things are looking good."

"We'd see each other all the time!" Megan said.

"School, church, home—it will be awesome!"

About a week later, the worry started to set in. Mom and Dad didn't seem to be moving to seal the deal on the cute house with the horseshoe driveway and had turned their attention to a far less favorable property.

"It's crazy!" I shouted into the phone receiver. "The walls are all sickly puke-yellow-green and the whole place smells of incense. They've got beads hanging in the doorways and idols everywhere. It's creepy!"

"What happened to the other house?" Megan asked. "The one *we* like?"

"Mom keeps saying it's too big," I said. "The puke house is smaller and newer and there's less to paint. The worst of it is that it's twenty minutes away. A whole new school zone."

"What are you going to do?"

"I don't know. I can't do the new-kid thing again. I just can't."

Weeks later, we moved into the garish beaded house that stood in the opposite direction from everything I wanted: Megan, the school we were going to attend together, and most of our friends. A twenty-minute car ride was almost insurmountable for someone without a driver's license.

One summer evening after Wednesday church, Megan and I finished our usual walk around the building and settled on a small concrete staircase by the rear entrance.

"I hate the new house," I said. I was angry that I wasn't walking to Megan's house every day, bitter about the disruption to our plans and the loss of the high school experience that should have been ours.

"I know," Megan said. Her voice became softer, quieter. "I had some bad news myself this week."

"Oh, no!" I said, "What happened?"

"My dad got this offer," her voice drifted. "To go to a new church."

My heart sank. Pastor Smith and his family at our church was one of the constants of my life. Their presence was an anchor—something I never questioned.

"It's a good opportunity," Megan was saying. "A really big congregation."

My mind was racing through the list of the bigger churches in the area, trying to figure out which one would have been most likely to want Pastor Smith.

"It's even on TV," Megan continued.

"TV?" My thoughts snapped to a standstill. I couldn't think of a single local church that televised their services.

"It's in Miami, Dani," Megan said, tears running down her face.

"Oh." I slumped over as my eyes filled with tears. It hadn't mattered where my family moved after all. High school with Megan was never meant to be.

A couple weeks later, I stood alongside Megan on the church stage and reached for her hand beneath her father's pulpit. In honor of the Smith family's last Sunday, we decided to sing the Michael W. Smith song "Friends." The anthem was firmly cemented in youth group culture—a go-to ballad reserved for going-away parties, graduations, and heart-wrenching farewells of all varieties. Tears drenched our faces as we sobbed our way through the chorus.

A few days later, Megan was gone. But not before she'd repeated her mantra one last time. "I'm still praying," she said. "If anything happens, I still want to be your girlfriend."

6

Unguarded

THINGS BEGAN TO CHANGE INSIDE the ugly house. Mom tore down the beaded doorway dividers, eliminated the lingering aroma of incense, and painted over the sickly shades of citrus. I decorated my room in homage to my obsession, Christian music sweetheart Amy Grant. My walls were covered in posters, and my bedspread was leopard print, intended to mirror the pattern of the thigh-length jacket she wore on the cover of her newest album, *Unguarded*.

But no amount of redecorating masked the emptiness inside *me*. I had simultaneously lost my best friend and first love, neighborhood, pastor, and, eventually, church. After the Smiths moved to Miami, the church, under new leadership, began a theological shift that my parents didn't like. They joined a new congregation that had neither a building nor teenagers. I thrived on social interaction, and suddenly, I had none. I began to withdraw into my room. When I emerged, I was sullen and short with my family.

"This isn't like you, Dani," Mom would say. "Tell me how you are feeling."

I would typically shrug in response, but one day my emotions exploded like a shaken two-liter of Pepsi.

"You want to know my feelings?" I screamed, tears pooling in the corners of my eyes. "I'll tell you how I feel. You ruined my life! I have no friends. And you don't care!"

Mom remained calm. "Dani, you know what we're going to do? We're going to pray about this. We're going to talk with Dad. We'll find something for you."

It wasn't just talk. Mom tore into action, gathering leads on various youth meetings at other churches. Dad drove me to all the different places, in hopes of hitting on something I would enjoy. I was a brutal critic.

"How did you like it?" Mom asked when I returned from a meeting one evening.

"I hated it. The kids were snobbish, the leaders didn't plan anything, and none of these groups you've taken me to are remotely close to what I had. I had something great, and you guys took it from me." It was harsh and I knew it. Of course my parents weren't responsible for the Smiths leaving, or for the direction the new church went afterward, but they were a safe target for my anger and frustration.

Although my parents didn't give up on finding a new youth group for me, they started making a point to keep me connected to my old church friends by inviting some of their families over for dinner. One night, it was Cadi's family. Cadi was two years older and sported long, straight brown hair, tight jeans, heavy metal T-shirts, and a racy reputation. She had been part of my broad social circle. Her friendship with Megan and Tess meant she always got invited to bigger events like my birthday sleepovers when Dad would draw on his youth leader skills and plan a full night of games and activities, but I never had a close, one-on-one friendship with her. After dinner, when the adults went to talk in the living room, Cadi and I were left with the task of finding common ground. It didn't take long for me to realize why Cadi and I had never connected.

"Want to listen to some music?" I asked.

Cadi shrugged. "What do you have?"

"I've got some Amy Grant, Michael W. Smith..." I started, and then paused as I took in the Iron Maiden T-shirt slit into a plunging V-neck and the cross necklace that skimmed just above the low point. "Or some DeGarmo and Key," I said, trying for something a little higher on the Christian music intensity scale.

"No Mötley Crüe, huh?" Cadi asked.

"Um, no. How about playing Pac-Man?"

"I don't like video games," Cadi said.

I mentally scrambled to come up with something else to suggest before settling on board games. I suggested a *Happy Days*–themed game and another from *Mad* magazine—time-tested staples I regarded as go-to crowd pleasers. Fortunately, these standbys didn't fail me. Soon Cadi and I were racking up "cool points" with the Fonz on Arnold's jukebox and sending tokens around the *Mad* board, with the goal of losing all of our paper "*Mad* money"—emblazoned with the iconic image of boyish mascot Alfred E. Neuman—in a sort of reverse Monopoly.

The games gave us a script of sorts, eliminating the need to invent conversation. As my stack of *Mad* money dwindled, the space between our chairs shrank as well. When Cadi would ask a question to clarify a rule, she'd touch my arm or brush a finger across my hand. If I didn't know better, I'd have thought she was flirting with me. I'd seen her do it with the guys at youth group for years: a flip of the hair, a coy smile, excessive touchiness. She was technically dating one of the youth group guys, but that didn't stop her from ducking into a closet or beneath a stairwell with any one of a large cast of boys.

Sounds from the living room indicated that the evening was winding down for the adults, so I didn't suggest a new game. I started boxing up the *Mad* money when Cadi suddenly said, "Hey, can I spend the night?"

I was taken aback. Sure, we'd gotten through the evening, but I didn't think we'd made enough headway to sustain an overnight. Still, I didn't feel like I was in a position to turn away friends. So I said, "Why not? Let's ask."

Once we were in my room, Cadi kicked off her padded pink-and-gray Reeboks and began to settle in. She was still acting funny—really touchy-feely. I was confused. I opened a drawer, pulled out a T-shirt, and tossed it in her direction. She disappeared down the hall. When she returned, I flipped the light switch and started toward bed, but Cadi reached out and kissed me full and hard on the lips. I was stunned, but not shy about returning her advances. My head was reeling—she really was flirting! I found the attention not only intrinsically thrilling—*a girl is kissing me!*—but even more exciting for what I assumed it meant: Cadi saw me—as myself, as male. Could this be the result of all my prayers? Was my transformation becoming fully effective? If Cadi saw me as a guy, would other people soon see too?

From that night on Cadi became a regular visitor at our house. Sometimes she came with her family for dinner or dessert and we would excuse ourselves to head toward the TV to watch *Miami Vice, Max Headroom,* or maybe *The A-Team,* depending on the day. During commercial breaks, I would ask about mutual friends at church and get caught up on all the news. We still didn't have much in common, except for a mutual interest in the sleepover that Cadi would always suggest at the end of the evening.

Our make-out sessions were long and frequent. Cadi got more daring as time went on, going so far as to lock lips with me in the backseat of our family car with Dad at the wheel, as we were taking her home after an afternoon movie at our house. I kept an eye on the rearview mirror, bracing myself for the moment when my father's eye would catch mine, or he'd slam on the brakes and pull the car to the curb, but it never happened—Dad either legitimately or intentionally never saw the passion playing out in the seat behind him.

Meanwhile, I was enjoying a normal teenage experience with Cadi. It wasn't exactly a romance—not in the talk-for-hours, heart-to-heart, you-really-get-me sense, like it was with Megan. It was simply physical. I didn't feel anything for Cadi. I didn't care when I'd hear, a day or so after a few stolen moments in my room, that she was in the church broom closet with another guy, or holding hands with someone else during youth group. But anytime we could get someplace private, Cadi would be all over me, sitting on me, kissing me—it was a heady experience. An ego boost. I didn't overthink it or let it go too far. I never questioned Cadi's interest in me, which I chalked up as proof that my prayers were working, that someone had finally seen me. And even though I may have been tempted to let my hand wander down from Cadi's face, I never gave in to the urge. I was petrified of getting into a situation where my own body would be exposed.

I was still emotionally invested exclusively in Megan. We may have been limited to letters and the occasional phone call, but I made the most of these tools. I was allowed to make one long-distance phone call per month, and I used the entire hour, but it was in print that I really shone. Ink issued from my pen like blood from a gaping wound. As far as love letters go, mine were suitable for Disney. Still, my words reflected sentiments that didn't exactly jive with the notion of correspondence between best girlfriends, an idea I never expected to have to justify until a phone session several months after the Smiths' move.

"Um, so something happened this week," Megan's voice came across the line just above a whisper.

"What's going on?"

"Mom found your letters in my room. She read them."

I felt flushed, nervous. "What did she say?"

"She said something's wrong with you—that you aren't quite right. She's really concerned."

I felt sick.

"Hey," Megan said. "It's okay. Just tone your letters down—don't be obvious."

My letters shifted into chatty, neutral territory. I was terrified of the possibility of Megan's parents forbidding further contact. I knew I had to change, to appear normal. I fortified an already near-impenetrable guard. I had been wrong in my hope that other people were beginning to see me as myself; I knew now that they still saw me as a freak. My secret wasn't safe. The truth about my body, about my identity, was something I had to hide. I couldn't let my guard down again—ever.

My connection with Cadi eventually fizzled. And my horror over Megan's mom's suspicions morphed into a glimmer of hope for redemption. A parent-approved plan was in the works for me to fly to Florida to surprise Megan. From Pastor and Mrs. Smith's perspective, the visit was more for Tess than Megan. Like me, Tess was having difficulty adjusting to the changes in her life, and a friendly face from home would bring a needed boost. I saved my allowance and began volunteering for extra chores—washing the car, pulling weeds—typical teenage money-making schemes. Several weeks later, the plan became reality: the ticket was purchased and arrangements were made for Mrs. Smith to pick me up at the Miami airport.

My traveling wardrobe was inspired by *Miami Vice*—one of my favorite shows. I wasn't specifically emulating either Crockett or Tubbs, but rather, the palette and panache of the eighties Miami fashion the drama showcased each week. I sauntered off the plane clad in a crisp white sport coat, linen khaki pants, and boat shoes. I was confident I'd arrived in Miami looking trendy, local, and masculine.

Mrs. Smith gave me a rundown on the plan as we claimed my baggage and headed to the car. "The girls are at the church now, at our weekly potluck. We should arrive just in time for you to go through the tail end of the line and then take a seat at their table," she said. "Tess will be so thrilled!"

I was more excited than nervous as the view from the car window became progressively affluent. Sure, I was happy to see Tess, but, more importantly, I was going to experience a week of life with Megan in her new environment. I'd go to school with her and hang out with her new friends, matching faces with the names I'd heard in her stories. It was a dream come true.

I skated through the potluck line plopping who-knew-what on my plate. My mind was on just one thing: sliding into the empty seat I'd scoped on the other side of the room—the one closest to Megan. My heart slammed inside my chest as I crossed the room. When my plate hit the table, I held my breath, waiting for my presence to register, for the reaction.

Megan's head turned upward and her eyes met mine. She blinked. "Oh. Wow. What are you doing here?"

Shock jolted through my system, but before the full impact registered, Tess bounded from her seat and gave me the greeting I wanted from Megan. "This is so awesome! I am so excited!" she screamed as she began introducing me to her friends.

Megan remained seated. In response to the raised eyebrows in her immediate circle, she simply said, "This is Dani, a friend from my old church."

I glanced around, sizing up my competition. The room teemed with attractive guys, all vying for Megan's attention. And she was doing her best to sustain their interest. The Megan at the table was a highly polished version of her former self, sporting styled, freshly highlighted hair and flawless makeup. She clung to her circle of high-end friends for the duration of the evening, but Tess stayed by me.

I hoped things would change the next morning—that after Megan adjusted to the shock of my sudden appearance and extracted herself from her throng of admirers, things would go back to normal. But I instantly felt like a tagalong during her school day, trailing Megan from class to class. Eventually I stopped trying to lighten the mood and just kept to myself. I discovered through overheard conversation that Megan had plans that evening with a group of her friends. I wondered if she'd invite me along, but she squashed that hope as soon as we arrived back at her house after school. "I'm sorry, Dani," she said, "but I have plans I made a while back. You'll be okay with Tess tonight, won't you?"

I nodded. What else could I do?

"I'll be out late, so I might not see you when I get home. Tomorrow morning we're carpooling to school with my friend, Lark DiMucci, so we need to be up and ready a little earlier, okay?"

"DiMucci?" I asked, immediately thinking of the singer Dion DiMucci, one of my sister Mary's favorite artists. She was forever playing "Trust in the Lord," a catchy song with a funky Caribbean beat. "Like Dion?" I asked Megan.

"Yeah, Dion is Lark's dad. He's driving us to school tomorrow."

She delivered the news casually, like it was a normal thing in her new life to be driven to school by one of last year's Grammy award nominees. Just a few short months ago, this would have been a big deal. It would have sparked hours of discussion. I missed those times.

The next morning, Dion pulled up in front of the house wearing the signature taxi-driver cap he'd sported in every picture I had ever seen of him. It was as though he'd walked off the cover of one of his albums and into my world. I slid into the backseat as Megan offered a quick introduction.

"I love your music! I have your tape right here!" I said, waving the cassette case I'd grabbed from the stash of trip music I brought along for my Walkman. "Would you sign it for me?"

Getting Dion's autograph was a bright spot in what continued to be a disappointing week. Everything I saw of Megan's new life revolved around fashion and image. Designer brands like Jordache jeans anchored her new, upgraded wardrobe. Tess was her old self at first, but things between us became strained as the visit wore on and my indifference and constant questions about Megan began to sting.

"She's changed," Tess shrugged. "She's one of the popular people." By the end of the week, I was relieved to be flying back home.

Things were never the same after the Florida visit. My letters slowed to a trickle and Megan's responses stopped altogether. It would be another year before I'd see Tess and Megan again—a year during which I held on to a thread of hope that when we met again, things would be different.

7
Goodbye

"I WANT TO COME AND pick you guys up in my new car," I said into the receiver. I hoped my voice sounded upbeat and casual, that the undertone of shakiness I was struggling to contain did not convey across the landlines. It was early summer, and Megan, Tess, and their parents had returned from Florida for a month-long visit with family. The news came from my parents; neither of the girls had been in touch. Perhaps one or two awkward communications had passed between us since I left Miami, and not a word about the visit.

It had taken days to manufacture the nerve to make this call. I needed the right pretense, the right "in" to the conversation. It finally arrived in the form of a coupon. JCPenney was offering free eight-by-ten portraits for a nominal sitting fee, a deal that gave me an anchor activity for what I hoped would turn into a full day at the mall with Megan and Tess.

"You have a car?" Megan was saying.

I pumped my fist in victory. Megan had asked a question—an invitation to keep talking. "Yeah, Mom and Dad got a new car after I had a little fender bender with the K-car. It was the other guy's fault. I inherited the Vega."

"That station wagon?" Megan said.

"Yeah! That bright yellow station wagon is now mine! And here's the best part," I said, drawing out the story with some dramatic tension. "It's not just a yellow Vega. It's the Amy Grant–mobile!" I grinned, nodding in affirmation as I revealed my car's moniker like it was the grand prize on a game show.

"Huh?" Megan said.

"Yeah, so I took two big *Unguarded* buttons and superglued them back-to-back as a mirror ornament," I said. "And—this is the best part—the only music allowed in the car is—of course—Amy Grant, *or* people associated with Amy Grant, like, say, Michael W. Smith or Reneé Garcia." I smiled broadly into the phone, bobbing my head up and down. "Like it?"

Megan laughed, but it sounded hollow. "So, about these pictures…Let's coordinate. I am thinking we all wear pink and white."

I swallowed hard. Pink and white was not the image I wanted to project. But for the moment, giving Megan what she wanted was more important than how I looked. This could be the last chance I had to win back my best friend, the person who, at least at one time, seemed to "get" me. I had to show her that things could be normal again. And if *normal* meant all three of us in pink and white, then that was the way things had to be for now.

"Okay," I said. "I'll pick you guys up in the morning and we'll do this."

I headed to the bathroom first thing the following morning, determined to put together a look that would put Megan at ease and make her feel like things would be okay—that we could get back to the way things were. During my tenure in the PE locker room, I had observed the round-brush-and-blow-dryer technique necessary to transform my mullet into the poofy "feathered" look that was in style. In the recesses of my closet, I found a pink shirt (a gift from a relative? one of Mary's castoffs?) and a pair of white pants. I rooted through a bathroom drawer, pulling out various compacts and tubes of stray makeup, and, drawing once again on locker-room observations, applied the contents. I took a long look in the mirror.

The image staring back wasn't mine, but I hoped it might match what Megan wanted to see. *Get the friendship recognizable first,* I told myself, *and worry about you later.* The eight-by-ten that resulted from this effort wasn't meant to be a displayable keepsake, anyway. It was the time I was really after. We just needed a reset, here, in Virginia, our home turf. This look I put together was just the price of readmission back into our friendship.

But the day I envisioned of bonding at the mall wasn't meant to be. The phone rang just as I was heading out the door to pick up the girls. Megan and

Tess arranged their own ride to the mall. They'd meet me at Penney's, pose for the picture, and then they had to go. They'd made other plans; they were sorry.

Despite the disastrous visit to Miami, it took seeing Megan again at home to comprehend that our friendship was truly gone. I saw the girls just one more time that summer at a church picnic both our families attended. Tess and I talked for a bit, but Megan kept her distance. It was clear that the JCPenney Portrait Studio had immortalized the defining friendship of my childhood at the exact moment of its death; me awash in Pepto pink and the sisters pausing to pay fleeting homage to the past before hurrying toward other plans, another future. Indeed, the three of us would never again be together, smiling, in one place. It was as though a sinkhole opened in the floor of the studio and simply sucked the friendship from my life.

8

Lifelines

I WAS HURT IN THE wake of Megan and Tess's final departure from my life, but two things kept me from complete despair in the summer of 1986. The first was a job. Not a typical burger-flipping gig, but actual summer mission work. A woman from church connected me with Child Evangelism Fellowship (CEF), an organization looking for Backyard Bible Club leaders for school children on summer break. "Host families" provided snacks and a backyard, and we'd invite neighborhood kids to come for a week of "club" sessions with games and stories that it was my job to lead. On Sundays I met my host families and canvassed the neighborhoods around their homes, passing out flyers for the event. Monday through Friday, I led three club meetings in three different neighborhoods for six weeks.

The second development that preserved my psyche that summer was finally landing a social life. I hadn't returned to public school, in part because of the cross-town move but also because homeschooling served me pretty well. My academic life was in good shape, but my social life remained abysmal until my parents broadened their search beyond churches. Although Dad was skeptical of groups that weren't attached to specific churches he knew and trusted, when he learned about Campus Life, he knew he had to let me try it.

The group focused on high school students from several area schools. It was designed to be a safe environment for teens to form relationships with peers and mentors who would encourage them in their faith. They played crazy, goofy games—things involving relays and sticky substances—that made me feel carefree again, more like myself. The few familiar faces I saw were friendly ones, acquaintances from my old neighborhood. The outlet became more than just a weekly gathering; it grew into a way of life. I saw the group as a place where outcasts found a home.

Soon I was going out after meetings and hanging out with the core group members and leaders at places like Burger King or Pizza Hut. Mike Stewart, the twenty-eight-year-old citywide Campus Life leader, was always a fixture at these after-parties. He circled the tables, checking in with his people, listening, making plans to meet up for lunch at the school cafeteria or to catch a concert or sporting event a student was involved in. Dark-haired, lanky, and perpetually dressed in a button-down shirt and crisp pants, Mike was soft-spoken and calming. I absorbed the cadence of his voice like music; whenever he spoke, I just wanted to listen. I admired Mike's ability to tell students that they were messing up while simultaneously building their self-esteem. He made people feel like they could change—like they could be better. He had a way of pinpointing students' strengths with laserlike precision.

One night Mike suggested that I might want to help out with the music during weekly meetings. Up to that point the guy in charge of music was, to my eye and ear, a carbon copy of John Denver. He leaned in on campfire ditties like "If I Had a Hammer," "Kumbaya," and "In the Jungle." Although the guy was only twenty, I'd pegged him as a decade behind his time and decided he could probably use a hand.

At first I filled out the sound as an extra guitar during song sessions at our meetings. Then John Denver started asking me to sing background here and there. Eventually I began suggesting new songs to try. John Denver told Mike he could use more of my help, and so I began going to a second night of Campus Life each week, on the other side of town. Between the two meetings, I was playing in front of two hundred students each week.

I began to cultivate a new look to correspond with my developing social life. Drawing inspiration from the popular punk scene, I grew my hair long in the back and trimmed it cropped and spiky at the top. I cut diagonals across my shirts and bought several pairs of Chucks that I mixed and matched at will: blue on one foot and yellow on the other one day, maybe red and blue the next. I tied a brightly colored bandanna around one of my denim-clad thighs and finished off the look with several chains that trailed from belt to my pocket. Other days I'd gravitate toward long striped shirts with flipped collars and finish off the look with a pair of *Max Headroom* sunglasses. I was honing my Campus Life persona to a fine point.

～✌～

"LET'S HEAD TO MIKE'S!" GINA'S voice came from the other end of the phone receiver.

"Be right there!" I said, hanging up and heading for the Amy Grant–mobile.

With school out, Campus Life was technically on summer hiatus, but Gina had introduced me to the constant party that was the Campus Life off-season.

After I'd gotten my license and commissioned the Amy Grant–mobile, I started transporting not only myself to group meetings but also Gina, a sporty, gap-toothed student. Gina knew how to have a good time, so when school ended, I was more than happy to keep driving both of us to restaurant meet-ups, forkings (cover-of-darkness events that involved pushing hundreds of plastic forks into the lawns of our unsuspecting friends or family), and the constant hangout taking place in Mike's living room. The space itself wasn't anything special—a two-bedroom pad with white walls, a sofa, and enough mismatched chairs to seat at least a dozen within view of a pretty nice TV and VCR setup—but the scene was welcoming and communal. It didn't take me long to realize that virtually anyone could walk through the door at any moment. Mike's apartment was a thriving, active set where our lives played out. Some predictable regulars anchored the scene: Karen and Deborah, Mike's longtime friends, both in their late twenties; Troy, also around twenty and popular with all the girls; and Dale, a big, boisterous guy with dark, bushy hair and a mustache who typically bumbled through the door with a bag of groceries and a diverse crowd of stragglers he'd picked up, seemingly from the streets.

I pulled into the parking lot of Mike's building and parked the Amy Grant–mobile. As we opened the door—no knocking here—a warm, spicy aroma told me Dale was already in the kitchen.

"Is that shrimp Creole I smell?" Gina asked.

"Oh, you know it!" Dale said, pausing what appeared to be a deep conversation with a guy who was perched on a stool watching him chop onions and celery. "Give it another half hour and we'll be in business."

"I've got my card right here if you want to see it," the guy said, reaching for his wallet. He held a laminated rectangular ID card up to my nose. "It's a residence card," he explained. "Until this afternoon, my address was the psychiatric hospital."

And now, here I was, about to eat shrimp Creole with a ragtag bunch of people crowded into Mike's two-bedroom apartment. It was as simple as that: wander in this door from anywhere and you find a home. I began to think of Mike's place as a refuge: not a place safe enough to share my secret—no place was that safe—but a place where I didn't need to act feminine or polished to feel at home.

As the summer wore on, I clung to my dual lifelines. I became a regular at Mike's apartment. No matter how many people were there or what was going on, Mike always found time for one-on-one moments with everyone. He'd ask me about my music. He wanted to know if I was writing songs (I was), what they were about (spiritual themes with a twist of angst), and if he could hear them (maybe). I eventually shared a single song with Mike. I'd written it while sitting on the sea wall at the beach one late-summer afternoon with thoughts of Megan skirting the periphery of my mind. I prayed for a while and then softly began to strum my guitar and sing,

There's something about that peace of mind
when the Lord's right by your side
he will take away your sorrow and wipe your eyes dry.
Take a moment now to think about God's awesome power
and to thank him for what he's done for you.

The song soothed me. From then on, peace washed over me every time I sang it. Mike's gentle encouragement probably had everything to do with that.

In fact, Mike encouraged everything I did.

"How is work going, Dani?"

No matter what part of my week I told him about—the Backyard Bible Club kids, the host families, or the lessons—his reaction was the same. "I'm really proud of what you're doing. You are becoming a real leader," he'd say.

The club sessions were much more than a summer job to me. I am sure the neighborhood kids enjoyed the games, snack, and story, but I found a role model. Three times each day I told the story of Mary Slessor, a strong, single, Scottish missionary and adventurer—and each time I did, I identified with her more.

Short, and red headed, with a squarish face more accurately described as handsome than pretty, Slessor physically resembled me in ways that, consciously or not, reinforced her image as a worthy model in my mind. In backyard after backyard, I described her adventures to groups of wide-eyed children: Mary sailing to Africa, Mary making a home in a Nigerian town where no other European had set foot, Mary rescuing twins left to die in the bush because they were thought to be demon spawn.

Mary lived among tribal people, mastered their language, ate their food, and earned enough trust that she was able to reverse many human rights violations that the tribe held as common mores, such as trial by poison to determine a suspect's guilt. She was brave and bold and did work that mattered—all alone.

I'd always loved the idea of Africa. I had devoured a book called *Escape to the Jungle*, a collection of adventurous missionary stories that captured my imagination. But Mary's life gave me something I could model. She was rough-and-tumble—doing things even men weren't doing. When she was surrounded by hippos in her canoe, she just hit them over the head with pots and pans. Nothing stopped her. She was a single woman unlimited by her gender and being effective for Christ.

To my teenage thinking, Africa seemed the way out of the mess I was in. On that continent it wouldn't matter who I was. In Mary, I began to see a model for celibacy, the potential to skirt the issue of romance in favor of ministry and adventure. I began consuming information about Africa, in search of my own jungle-esque place to escape. When I came across a magazine article about Benin being in need of missionaries, my future seemed set. West of Nigeria, where Mary's work played out, the country of Benin seemed a suitable corollary. Finally I had found answers. I began mentally preparing for a life in Africa.

WHEN CAMPUS LIFE STARTED UP again in the fall, I threw myself into ministry full force. The John Denver doppelgänger didn't return, so Mike asked me if I'd be interested in doing all the music for both groups' weekly meetings.

"Technically, it's against the rules for you to serve in leadership since you haven't graduated yet," Mike said. "But since you aren't in public school, no one really knows. I'd like for you to do it."

I embraced the opportunity as my new purpose, perhaps even as training for my future life in Africa. I would be singularly devoted to ministry now. Before, I had been preoccupied with worry over whether it was okay for me to like women, let alone pursue them. Over time, I had learned subtle ways to push connections with girls, and it wasn't just Megan and Cadi who had responded. I often felt what I assumed to be normal male-female chemistry with girls I was attracted to—girls I knew liked men. My thinking was that if a girl got to know me, she would instinctively—magically perhaps—know me for who I was. If they like guys, I reasoned, then they would like me. I learned to play with proximity, gauge interest, and see if I could tease out a flirtatious response. Girls would often seem surprised, but it wasn't unusual for them to respond, reach for my hand, flirt back, and treat me like I had seen them treat other guys.

My view was one-dimensional. I so thoroughly identified as male that it was hard for me to view myself outside my skin—to see myself as others did, in the feminine. That's why it was always so jarring when I would hear comments like, "You're gay," or "You're a dyke," which happened sometimes even in the Campus Life environment. I knew it couldn't possibly be true. I'd been told repeatedly that being gay was a sin, shameful, wrong. I wasn't that kind of person. No way. I don't know for sure how many of those rumors came back to Mike, but I knew Mike understood that something different was going on with me. I also knew that Mike supported me anyway. Every now and then, he'd say, "You're just being yourself, and that's great."

I began learning to be okay with being myself, at least for the moment. Dating had proven too confusing. It seemed I would have to cut it out of my life if I was going to devote myself to ministry. My involvement with Campus Life soon extended beyond the two meeting nights each week. I began to go with Mike to schools during lunch to eat with the students, building rapport and friendship. I was consumed by Campus Life. The students, the meetings, the music—these things made up my world.

In the spring I was selected to go to Washington, DC, for a weekend leadership conference with some Campus Life people. Days before our departure, I was felled by a stomach bug, but I never wavered from my determination to go. The trip was a big deal to me. There was no way I was going to miss it. That Friday afternoon, I boarded the fifteen-passenger van and shut down my overactive intestines with the force of medicine and sheer will. Mike was supposed to go, but he got sick at the last minute and, unlike me, had bowed out.

In DC, Gina—my roommate—and I got settled into our hotel room and quickly jumped into the evening program. It wasn't until late that night, after things were winding down, that Troy finally showed up at the convention center. Troy, the good-looking guy who'd been a summertime fixture at Mike's house and right hand at meetings throughout the school year, had dropped out last-minute from the van, announcing without explanation that he would drive himself and meet up with the group later. I didn't think much of it until I saw his face, now, as he approached the group. One look at his drained expression communicated bad news: something was seriously wrong.

"It's Mike," he said, once the group gathered. "He's in the hospital. I don't have much information, but he's really sick. We need to pray."

I struggled to process the words. It seemed impossible that Mike could be sick enough to be hospitalized, let alone critical. I'd just seen him the night before. He seemed pretty normal, aside from what I assumed was a cold. I went through the rest of the conference mechanically: outwardly moving, appearing in the right places at the right times, processing nothing.

The ride home from DC was tense. When we pulled into the church parking lot, I saw Mike's friends Karen and Deborah waiting, their faces streaked with tears.

I processed the next few moments through the few disjointed phrases that penetrated the pounding in my ears.

"He's gone."

"Sick for a long time."

"Heart condition."

"Transplant list."

"Excited to be with Jesus now."

Shock jolted through my body as my mind argued: *I just saw him. He had a cold. He never, ever mentioned being sick.*

I somehow ended up at home, in bed, cognizant of nothing until the moment when I stood once again in front of a church congregation choking back sobs, this time strumming my guitar while I sang:

There's something about that peace of mind
when the Lord's right by your side
he will take away your sorrow and wipe your eyes dry.
Take a moment now to think about God's awesome power
and to thank him for what he's done for you.

9
Melissa

AFTER MIKE'S DEATH, THE CAMPUS Life gang remained active, even without the cohesion of the off-season home base of his apartment. I spent a lot of time with Gina and her friend Melissa. I hadn't liked Melissa at first; she was loud and opinionated—the type of person I guess you either liked or you didn't. I found her downright obnoxious. But since both Melissa and I spent so much time with Gina, proximity caused my feelings to change. I began to see her as bubbly and talkative, and we became good friends.

Melissa developed a crush on a guy named Tim. He asked her out to a concert, but she didn't want to go out with him alone—so she asked me to come along as a date for Tim's friend Doug. I figured it was just for one night. Doug and I would be extra wheels on a date that was really all about bringing Melissa and Tim together. Besides, the tickets were for Sheila Walsh, the Pat Benatar of Christian music—and I could see her live for free: Why not?

The evening began with a mutual friend from our crowd serving the four of us a homemade lasagna dinner at her apartment. I was wearing my typical out-on-the-town style: khaki pants, boat shoes, and a pink-and-white-striped shirt. My hair was molded into a dramatic swoop in the front that parted somewhere around the intersection of David Bowie and A Flock of Seagulls.

Doug was an easygoing guy with an athletic build; close-cropped, dirty-blond hair; and brown eyes. I envied his look. I had been spending time bodybuilding at home and figured I was probably Doug's equal in strength. But Doug pulled off the traditionally masculine image that I wanted for myself.

Over dinner, I discovered that Doug was a lot of fun. We shared an interest in sports, and conversation flowed naturally. Meanwhile, Melissa and Tim were hitting it off as well. The group felt solid to me. By the time the concert was over and I found myself sitting in Shoney's next to Doug with one of the chain's brownie desserts between us—two square fudgy cakes separated by a layer of vanilla ice cream and doused in gooey syrup and whipped cream—I realized this one-time favor might extend well beyond the evening.

Melissa caught my eye from across the table, sending the unmistakable message: *This has got to happen!* That's when I realized how happy I could make everyone by settling into a relationship with a boyfriend. Doug was enjoyable to be around, and we seemed to have a lot in common. Perhaps I could stomach this—make it work. And that's how I became the reluctant girlfriend of a Navy sailor stationed at the Norfolk naval base.

From that night on, the four of us were inseparable. Melissa and Tim became a couple. Whenever they went out, it was assumed that Doug and I would go too: trips to the mall, dinner out, Putt-Putt golf, an evening at a traveling carnival, and Fourth of July on the beach. I was having a good time, even though I thought of the outings as fun times with friends—unless someone asked if I had a boyfriend. Then I'd pull out a picture of Doug and take in the smiles and nods of approval. Having Doug in my back pocket gave me an instant answer to the question that perpetually dogged me. Yes, I could now say, "I have a boyfriend." Box checked.

But the outward image of me as Doug's girlfriend didn't match what was happening on the inside, which was an ever-growing attachment to Melissa. We had long, emotional conversations about the biggest thing we had in common: grieving for Mike. Melissa had been an active Campus Life member until she became pregnant, engaged, and suddenly single again after she suffered a pregnancy loss.

Mike made it clear that it didn't matter to him what Melissa had done or where she had been: he just wanted her to come back, to join them again—to be with people who loved her. He never gave up and continued checking up on her periodically right up until his death. She was tormented by the memory of his last phone call, just weeks before he died: Mike being Mike, extending love and grace, and Melissa dismissing him outright: "Thanks, but I'm just not coming back."

"I just feel so guilty," she'd tell me. She had been close to Mike, part of the inner circle. He stood by her unconditionally, and she walked away. There was nothing she could do to make things right, so she poured her feelings out to me in long, tear-filled conversations. The raw emotion that fueled these talks was a powerful bonding agent: I was growing closer to Melissa than I had been with anyone since my time with Megan.

Seeing Melissa within the context of her relationship with Tim added another level of complexity for me. Watching her flirt with Tim made me see her not just as a friend but a woman—a woman I was becoming increasingly attracted to. I knew those feelings were supposed to be for Doug, but I felt repulsed by his attempts to physically advance our relationship. Doug was pressing me for alone time—dates that didn't involve Melissa and Tim. He began to come over to our house to watch TV with my family. These visits were torture. Everything about being alone with Doug felt unnatural, wrong. I kept reminding myself how happy this made everyone, how relieved my mother must have felt seeing me sitting at Doug's side. This was good; this was right, I told myself.

Sunday afternoon was a big hangout time at our house. Friends dropped by constantly, and soon that included Doug. One Sunday, everyone was watching TV in the living room. I sat stiffly next to Doug, fighting waves of anxiety roiling through my stomach. Doug inched in closer to me on the couch, but I subtly crept back into safer territory on the other side of the cushion. Undeterred, he slid his arm along the top of the sofa and slowly circled it around my shoulders. I cringed inwardly, and possibly outwardly as well. I couldn't wait for Doug to leave. When he finally did, I made a beeline toward my room, but Mom intercepted me on the way.

"Dani," she began, brow furrowed. "Can I talk with you for a second? I'm a little concerned."

I stopped in my tracks, wondering what was up.

"I just don't know about this guy, Dani. I don't really like what I'm seeing. You know, physically."

I froze, stunned. What had she *seen*? What *could* she have seen? My siblings full-on made out with their boyfriends and girlfriends in broad daylight in that very living room. What could she have witnessed in my unyielding posture to give her pause?

But this is for you! my thoughts screamed. How dare she not like the boyfriend I endured solely for her benefit? Mom's reservation was all the impetus I needed to break up with Doug. What could I do? My parents didn't approve. Later, I learned from Melissa that Doug told Tim the "ice queen" had broken up with him. I was thrilled with the title, glad there had been no confusion.

By fall, Melissa and Tim were no longer dating, and my friendship with Melissa deepened. We became emotionally dependent on each other in ways that were evident to our friends and my family.

Friends would make comments: "You guys need to be careful," or "Your relationship is dangerous."

Mom chimed in too. "This isn't healthy," she said.

The opposition only strengthened my attachment to her. It wasn't long before the relationship became physical, although it didn't go beyond making out. I was still determined never to get myself into a position that would expose my body.

"I don't understand what's happening," Melissa would say. "I'm not gay."

"I'm not either," I assured her. "That's not what this is." In my mind, this was enough information. My word had to be good enough: I wasn't gay. Melissa knew she wasn't gay either. To my thinking, it was the simplest of equations. If she felt attracted to me, she'd figure it out. She'd recognize me for who I was, but it was her responsibility to connect those dots. I wasn't willing to risk being a freak. "Let's keep what we have private," I said. "It's just between us."

Of course, this reasoning made no sense outside my head. Melissa didn't understand what was happening, but she wanted to. She trusted me. Despite her confusion, she agreed to keep the intimate details of our relationship private.

Meanwhile, Melissa and I poured most of our spare time into working with Troy, who had taken Mike's place at the helm of Campus Life leadership. The year before Mike died, we'd held meetings at two locations for a combined two hundred students, but now the meetings had dwindled to one location with just fifty attendees. We decided to dig into what we viewed as a rebuilding year. Melissa and I started a 5:00 a.m. girls' Bible study at one of the schools. I worked with Troy during the day, visiting a regular circuit of cafeterias for lunch with students. We weren't above gimmicks to get kids in the door. Troy and I promised that we'd each swallow a live goldfish if the meeting's attendance reached one hundred. Our efforts had some impact; I sent a fish slithering down my esophagus by midyear.

My life may not have quite added up, but I didn't think too hard about it. I liked Melissa. She liked me. We weren't gay. We couldn't be gay; it was impossible. Being gay was a sin—and besides, I was a guy. Everything was fine. We would just have to continue being careful until God worked out the details.

One night, Melissa and I were having a sleepover with our friend Jeanette. We were up pretty late, but once things settled down, I remained still in my bed, eyes wide open, listening for Jeanette's rhythmic breathing. When I was sure she was asleep, I padded over to Melissa's bed, where she was waiting for me. Our lips locked into a long, passionate kiss.

"What's going on?" Jeanette's voice broke the silence and the mood. Fear shot through my veins. Jeanette had only feigned sleep. She felt suspicious of Melissa and me and wanted to see what would happen.

My heart pounding, I scrambled to assure Jeanette that she didn't see what she thought she saw; that we weren't gay. And since we weren't gay, could she keep what she thought she saw to herself?

Jeanette agreed and was as good as her word for the rest of the school year. After the sleepover, life continued as normal: Melissa and I led our Bible study, I continued to help Troy connect with students, and Melissa was plagued with occasional pangs of guilt over the physical aspect of our relationship. When summer came, Melissa and I went separate ways: she went to camp and I took off for California with my parents to visit my oldest brother, Rick, who lived in California and had recently been divorced. As I boarded the plane, I had no way of knowing that the home I'd return to in two weeks would seem as unfamiliar as the place I was heading toward.

"Jeanette was here." I heard my sister Mary's voice over the phone. The words didn't alarm me at first; our house was a hub of activity, and my friends would often drop by whether I was home or not. Still, her tone was off. "She told Jim and I this afternoon that you're gay; that she saw you kissing Melissa." Horror washed over me as I heard my sister's voice narrating my worst nightmare.

With those words, my life hurled into chaos. I arrived home to discover that I had more to worry about than just the surface damage of Jeanette's broken promise. For the first time in our relationship, Melissa flew into full-on damage control instead of channeling opposition into strengthening our bond. Fresh from the sermons, prayers, and soul-searching that came with Christian camp, Melissa decided that she was done with me. She began telling our friends that I was gay; that I had made advances toward her. The stories that got back to me were unified: I had kissed Melissa. Not Melissa and I kissed each other.

I was hurt but still all in on the relationship. I saw it as salvageable—something that could be worked out. I kept calling her, begging to talk, but she was angry and every conversation turned vicious. "I need time away from you," Melissa said. "I don't even know if we can be friends."

I sank into a days-long depression.

"We told you this relationship wasn't healthy," Mom said in response to my funk. "Now you see why."

Then Troy asked me to lunch. "I don't care what happened," he said. "I just want to know where you stand. Are you gay?"

"Nope. I am 100 percent not gay." I leaned hard into my circular thinking: *I am not gay, so this didn't happen. There's no problem here.*

"Okay," Troy said, taking my words at face value. "Do you think you can still lead Bible study with Melissa under these conditions?" I told him I could.

~✏~

COME SEPTEMBER, BOTH MELISSA AND I showed up to our 5:00 a.m. group amid whispers:

"Dani's gay."

"How can they work together?"

"What even happened?"

Perhaps due to the tension, an increase in attendance, or a combination of the two, it wasn't long before the group split: half of the girls went with Melissa, the other half with me.

My roster was a mix of familiar faces and new recruits, one of which was Joanna, a student who began coming to evening meetings around the time of the ill-fated sleepover. I found Joanna annoying. She obsessed over perfect hair, trendy clothes, and accessories—like the collection of colorful and hard-to-find Swatches circling her arm. I saw her behavior as attention-seeking. Despite growing up in a single-parent household, Joanna nurtured the assumption that she came from money. In my mind, she cultivated the rich-girl image to mask the insecurity of being an overweight teen.

If there was any doubt that Joanna was my least favorite student, it became impossible to ignore one evening early that fall. I was shuffling around the house feeling sad and sulky about my falling out with Melissa when Mom issued a challenge.

"You need to get out of the house," she said. "What about the students in your discipleship group? You should be investing in the people you are supposed to be leading."

I knew Mom was right, so I began calling the girls in my group. Call after call, the result was the same: no one was home. Eventually, a single name remained on my list—Joanna. I dialed her number as a begrudging afterthought. To my disappointment, she answered the phone. She seemed nervous—I would find out later that she shook her head back and forth in a vigorous *no* when she covered the mouthpiece and asked her mother for permission to go out—but eventually agreed to go get dinner.

I picked up Joanna and headed to the Rock-Ola Café, an American-fare restaurant with a round neon sign resembling a vinyl record album. The eatery was a popular gathering place for Campus Life leadership. Once I overcame my misgivings about the evening and the initial awkward attempts at conversation, I began to relax. The next thing I realized, I was laughing—a lot. By the time the evening was over, I was sure of two things: I'd misread Joanna, and the time with her was something I needed.

Our friendship took off that night. Most mornings began with Joanna slipping me a handwritten note at our group study, telling me about her life, how comfortable she felt around me, how she could tell me anything. But of course, in Joanna's mind, I was a platonic, female girlfriend. "You're my best friend," she would say. "You're the only one I can trust."

Melissa seethed with disapproval as the relationship developed. "You need to be careful," she told me. Her words didn't register as concern for Joanna as much as jealousy. But Melissa didn't need to worry: my guard was at fortress strength. Joanna may have felt comfortable declaring that we were best friends, but that was no longer a designation I was assigning to anyone. Ever. No best friends.

Joanna was confused by my refusal to be her best friend, especially since we did everything together. I drove her around in the Chevy Sprint her mother had given her despite the fact that she was too young to drive. I was happy to be behind the wheel, especially since the Amy Grant–mobile had succumbed to a blown gasket that spring. I was enjoying my time with Joanna, but I wasn't willing to label what we had or count on it.

One night in mid-October, we went to a concert. As soon as I got back home, I was on the phone again with Joanna.

"I don't get the best friend thing," she said. "You don't want to label our friendship because you got hurt?"

I had to admit that my attempt at being a lone wolf was failing miserably. I spent all my time with this girl. "Okay," I relented. "From today forward, you are officially my best friend."

And thus began the relationship that would, fifteen years later, become my first marriage.

10

Marriage

WE SAID OUR VOWS ON a Thursday night in December 2003, with no one but God as our witness. There was nothing legal about our union, but that didn't make it any less real. Not that any path to a legal marriage existed, even if our relationship had been known to anyone other than the two of us.

I chose that Thursday to propose to and marry Joanna because it was her thirtieth birthday. Also, because we had rather recently crossed a major barrier between us that made our commitment feel right. Joanna and I had been sharing our lives together for fifteen years, but it had only been a matter of weeks since she truly knew me—as a man. In those fifteen years, Joanna had followed me to Bible college in Chicago and I had followed her back to Virginia to live with her and her mother, Momma Miller, in the house Joanna called home every day of her life. We also became colleagues, working alongside Momma Miller at her accounting firm. Spiritually, we were ministry partners, coleading youth groups at various churches over the years. In my mind we were a couple, but Joanna, like my past love interests, struggled with guilt over the attraction she felt toward me. Physically, I still hadn't done more than make out with anyone, and guilt racked Joanna's conscience every time we kissed.

Early in our relationship I followed my typical pattern of brushing aside any reservations Joanna expressed. It went beyond fear—although I was still terrified—or stubborn refusal. I truly believed the facts spoke for themselves: Joanna wasn't gay, and she liked me—in my mind, the only conclusion to draw was the obvious: I was male. I found any other suggestion emasculating:

I liked women because I was a man. Period. Expecting people—
especially girls—to simply understand my inherent maleness had
been the central issue of my life since I was that red-haired toddler
refusing to wear a green frilly dress. I was a college graduate with
hair that had long since faded to brown, still lying awake far into
the night hoping and praying that my friends and family would
simply understand—that they'd see me as the man I was. It was
wishful thinking, rooted in the desire for an easy way out of my
impossible circumstances. It was a best-case scenario that would
allow me to be myself without the risk of breaking the news and
losing everything.

What actually happened was a long trail of rumors and widespread,
whispered assumptions that I was gay. Although I'd rallied against that perception
for years, I slowly abandoned the anti-gay belief system I'd been taught and
eventually learned to let others live with their assumptions. It was easier that
way. Besides, I no longer believed that gay people were evil, so the *I-can't-be-gay-
because-gay-is-evil-and-I-am-not-evil* narrative no longer held sway.

What was difficult, though, was Joanna's perception of me. We'd make
out, and she would cry. "This is wrong," she'd say. "It has to stop!"

"Why is it wrong? I'm not gay. You're not gay." I was eighteen and had
been having versions of this conversation with Joanna for nearly two years. It
was so exhausting that I finally decided to explain myself with what I
considered graphic clarity: "There's something I want you to know about me,"
I said. "I'm different down there. I have both." There. I'd said it. Now she knew.

"Okay," Joanna said, nodding.

I paused, waiting for follow-up questions, but none came. *Wow! She's fine
with it! She understands and accepts me!*

I thought our relationship would be solidified by my admission, but in
this, I was disappointed. In fact, it seemed like absolutely nothing changed.
Some days were great; others were awful. We were together—but not really.
She occasionally pursued other guys. What was most confusing to me was

that she would still occasionally break down in tears after making out with me.

"I'm sorry," she'd say. "I just feel so guilty."

"Why?" I was incredulous. "I don't understand. What do you feel guilty about?"

The conversations ran in circles and ended only in confusion. I resigned myself to the role of Joanna's companion—a placeholder in her life until she found someone and got married.

And then, on April Fools' Day 2003, everything changed.

I had surgery that morning—my fourth at that point—for chronically terrible knees. The doctor performing my first surgery, which I'd had when I was in college, informed me that I had the knees of a retired pro football player but in my early twenties. Joanna and I were on the couch, my leg propped up and her thumb on the TV remote, when we stumbled on a documentary that had us instantly transfixed.

The documentary was about trans people: their lives, the transition process—one guy even looked a lot like me. Then came a segment about an intersex person and I saw the spark of understanding in Joanna's eyes the second it happened. "Wait! Are you telling me... are you...?" She paused as she stumbled over her words. "Are you telling me this is who you are?" She was elated, energized, utterly floored by the revelation.

"Yeah," I said. "I thought you knew!" I was baffled. Why she never asked more questions or why she continued to stay I do not understand fully to this day. All I knew is in that moment, everything clicked and she knew: she was attracted to me because I'm male.

I proposed in December, on her birthday. We had already decided to throw a huge party. Joanna had decided that if she was never going to have a wedding, she may as well throw a huge milestone birthday party. We had rented a venue, arranged a live band, and made a guest list of friends and family. In the wake of our private nuptials, we decided that the event would now double as our secret wedding reception. And in our minds, that's exactly what it was—even though no one congratulated us, bought us Crock-Pots, or took traditional photos of us. Why would they? From our guests' perspective, they were attending a birthday party. They came and left with no inkling that anything had fundamentally changed in the life of the birthday girl, let alone her best friend.

⋅⋅⋅

I WAS EXCITED TO FINALLY be having sex, but I was also experiencing more changes "down there"—unwelcome ones. I began having pain and discomfort that plagued me to a point I could no longer ignore. My luck had run out; I had to make an appointment. I had lived for more than thirty years without a doctor—let alone a gynecologist—examining my genitalia. I avoided the traditional baseline gyno exam when I was eighteen by promising my mother I'd go when I was twenty-one. When I became a legal adult, I simply never made the appointment. I continued the same wellness program that carried me through my adolescence: prayers for good health. I didn't sleep the night before the appointment, plagued by the thought that my whole world was about to change. I was convinced that the doctor would take one look and announce that I needed to be fixed; I'd be outed as a freak. Consumed by fear and worry about what the day would bring, I prayed through the night.

No scenario I imagined came close to what actually happened. I got up on the table and the doctor proceeded to do the exam without commentary. Even the fact that he had to use the smallest speculum to force his way into the tiny vaginal opening behind my testicle did not prompt a single inquiry. The doctor simply ignored the male genitalia and homed in on the parts he was trained to care for. I would later learn that my experience wasn't unusual; other intersex people have similar stories. I was sent on my way with nothing but some medication. I don't know if I was more relieved or baffled.

⋅⋅⋅

SHORTLY AFTER OUR MARRIAGE, JOANNA and I began attending the Inlet, a small, ragtag church in an old warehouse. The congregation drew from people on the fringes: economically, socially, spiritually—on both ends of the bell curve. Joanna and I found ourselves there after our old church got a new pastor and he sidelined us for being women in ministry—a conservative no-no. The Inlet wasn't concerned about our genders, and although people may have had their suspicions about our relationship, no one said anything. We began working with the teenagers, and it wasn't long before the teens and the ministry defined our social circle. Church services, youth events, and softball games rounded out my world.

Our social network at the Inlet also gave us ample opportunity to host former students and displaced friends in the guesthouse behind our home. One summer, it was Madi, a recent graduate. Confused about her sexuality, she needed a place to stay while she figured things out. Joanna and I were both excited. We loved Madi and enjoyed her company. As the summer wore on, though, Madi began to spend more time with me than Joanna. When summer ended and Madi went back to school, we stayed in close contact. The friendship had become important to me.

When Joanna realized Madi and I were developing a friendship outside of our threesome and that we were having frequent conversations that did not include her, she insisted that I make a phone call. Right then and there on our back patio, Joanna watched as I punched Madi's number into my phone. With tears rolling down my cheeks, I told Madi that we couldn't talk anymore, that we couldn't have a friendship that didn't include Joanna.

I was heartbroken: Madi was deeply depressed, and I felt like I deserted her. My guilt compounded the loneliness I felt after Madi left. Joanna felt threatened by any friendship I formed with a female, and men did not naturally include someone they saw as an overweight, butch woman in their social circles. My parents had taken on a role doing substitute mission work, and they were gone for months at a time. Without them there to serve as the hub, family gatherings were infrequent; I had gravitated more to Joanna's family and their traditions. Slowly, Joanna became my sole connection to the outside world, and I began suffocating in isolation. It wasn't as though I wanted my marriage with Joanna to fail. It just did.

Successful marriages are never guaranteed even in the best of situations—
but a closeted relationship with no external recognition or support was its
own kind of torture. The thing about closeted relationships is that they are
insular, sealed in layers of secrets that eventually form a tomb. Our union
never basked in the glow of public celebration, was never recognized or
validated by our inner circle. Our joys weren't known, our problems weren't
shared, and our very existence together was continually questioned.

I hung on for years, hoping Joanna would show me genuine attention.
Meanwhile, both Joanna and Momma Miller were financially dependent on
my paycheck. The accounting business had long since been sold, and I got a
good job as a controller in a corporate startup. I even took Joanna to Europe
in a last-ditch attempt to reconnect as a couple, but there were no sparks. We
had fun as friends by day and retired to separate beds at night. Following the
trip, I felt increasingly trapped and hopeless. Joanna was the only person who
knew my secret, and she had the power to ruin my world. But the coping
strategies I had relied on for so long had stopped working. I craved love and
genuine connection but no longer saw fulfillment as a possibility. Life was
becoming a duty I didn't think I could carry out much longer.

11

Risk

THE TRAFFIC DURING THE SUMMER of 2013 was worse than any I could recall before or since. The morning commute was tolerable, but the drive home was typically a two-hour crawl along hot asphalt. For the first time, I had a carpooling partner. Holding up my end of the conversation was awkward, despite being happy to have company for the unpredictable commute, which included the daily bottleneck at the Hampton Roads Bridge-Tunnel and an influx of summer traffic.

One of our former students and a good friend of Joanna's had returned home from college for the summer and became the latest guesthouse resident. But she also needed a summer job. Joanna asked me to find her an internship placement at my company—which I did. She also asked me to let her ride along to work every day. Krista had always been closer to Joanna than me. But although she was barely five foot three, she was bold, direct, and sassy in a way I found refreshing. She didn't play around with small talk, and it wasn't long before she started using the time in the car to introduce thought-provoking, open-ended questions that typically began with the phrase, "What do you think about..."

I'm the one who usually asks these questions, I thought. Even more intriguing was the fact that despite our age difference—despite the fact that she used to be a student in our youth program—Krista challenged me spiritually. She was a religious studies major and tough questions didn't scare her; she wasn't afraid of the answers. As I began to engage in these daily conversations, I felt more alive than I had in a long time—less isolated; more like myself. Less like giving in to the darkness that had been tugging at my mind, whispering the notion that everything would be better if I weren't around anymore.

"How can I pray for you?" Krista asked in the middle of one of our conversations.

The question threw me off guard. No one asked me things like that.

"It's obvious to everyone that you're struggling," Krista said. "Something's not right."

I don't know if it was that specific question or an overall increase in my comfort level, but I began to open up by degrees. In the early days of carpooling, Krista and I took turns playing our favorite songs and talking about what each one meant to us. One evening, with the car at a standstill near a park where the commute frequently stalled out, I cued up Plumb's "Cut."

Krista told me she had struggled with self-harm in the past, and I knew she'd find the song relatable. She opened up a bit about her experience, but she stopped. Something in my face must have given me away. Did I subconsciously get myself into this conversation on purpose? "What are you thinking?" Krista asked.

"I can relate to those feelings too," I said. "Just wanting to be numb … to turn off the whole world. To stop giving people what they want to see all the time." I didn't elaborate further, but the shared common ground emboldened me to ask Krista what her stance was on the LGBTQIA+ community.

"I don't really have an opinion," Krista said. "I just know that God seems to put a lot of people in my life, and he's calling me to love them—and that's exactly what I am going to do." She seemed taken aback by the question—almost surprised by the idea that she should have a preconsidered stance on who it was okay to love. I was feeling safe and heard for the first time in years. Forming an honest, healthy relationship with another human felt like a lifeline, but it was also a red flag.

I knew the terror welling inside me would make no sense to Krista, but the scenario playing out triggered memories of Madi's departure years earlier.

I had to do something to try to head off disaster. I knew I couldn't survive another severed friendship.

"I need to ask you to get closer with Joanna," I said. We were stuck in our afternoon commute when I took my eyes off the solid line of idling cars and glanced over at Krista.

She looked back in confusion.

"This friendship has to be a triangle. It's not going to work otherwise." I tried to imagine what the urgency and insistence in my voice sounded like to Krista.

"I don't understand. We're all friends, right?"

"If you were in my head, you'd understand," I said. "I can't tell you."

I was willing to risk sounding like an idiot if it meant a chance to keep Krista's friendship. Losing this connection was not an option for me, not when it was our conversations that gave me a reason to get up every day. Not when I knew that this friendship was keeping me alive.

Krista was confused, but she assured me that she would spend some time with Joanna if that would help me. And for now, that was enough.

MY MENTAL HEALTH MAY HAVE been fragile, but my physical health was in danger too. I was deteriorating rapidly: severe pain and massive bleeding became part of my daily life. Joanna insisted that I needed to see a gynecologist. She did some research and went alone on an investigative visit to a doctor who sounded like a promising fit.

"I really think this is the guy for you," Joanna said. My need for medical care was overcoming my fear and skepticism, so I agreed to go. As relieved as I had been at not being outed during my sole gynecological exam years earlier, my failing health demanded a consultation with someone better equipped to help.

Dr. H was that doctor. He understood immediately that I was intersex, but he was interested in more than the medical facts. He explained to me for the first time the toll being intersex was taking on my health. I was in pain and bleeding because my female organs were shutting down, but Dr. H didn't see that as my main problem.

"I am worried about your quality of life. You aren't living as who you are, and it's not healthy emotionally, physically, or spiritually. If you identify with your male side, why are you living as a woman?"

The answer was simple: I was living as a woman out of fear of losing faith and family, forces that were each difficult to overcome on their own, but that together formed a nearly insurmountable barrier. I certainly wasn't in top health, but I wasn't ill enough to risk my most foundational relationships.

"You talk about the importance of your faith and family," Dr. H said. Concern flashed across his face. "Don't you think they'll understand if you talk with them?"

"No," I said. "I don't."

There was no doubt. I mentally rewound to the summer Madi came to live in our back house.

"How are things going?" my mother asked one day, looking for an update.

"Madi's great. We're having fun."

"No, I mean what are you doing to help her out, spiritually?"

I sighed. Of course, I'd known all along this was the real question, just like I knew that Mom's definition of helping Madi "spiritually" meant making her straight.

"You know that Linda and I hoped Madi's summer with you would be a time of impact," Mom said. Madi's mother, Linda, was the reason Madi needed somewhere to stay in the first place, having told her daughter to leave the house if she was going to be a lesbian. Mom was the friend Linda turned to as her confidant, soliciting prayers, advice, and help in the form of Joanna and I as youth leaders who could steer her back on track.

"It's tragic what's happening to that family," Mom continued. "You need to be nudging her in the right direction."

If the message that I was failing as a spiritual leader was clear then, when Madi was trying to figure out her sexuality, it was amplified when the contemplation was over and Madi transitioned to Marty, a trans man.

Finally at peace in an identity that felt right, Marty began raising funds for top surgery: a procedure that would not just remove Marty's breasts, but shape the area into a more masculine form.

"Please, Dani," Mom said. "Talk to her. This surgery ... it's not something you can reverse."

"I am not going to discourage him, Mom. I am not comfortable with that."

"Linda's praying so hard against these fundraisers, that the money won't come together. This isn't something you can come back from, Dani."

And when you can't come back, what are you but lost? That was the tragedy Linda—and my mother—saw in Marty's transition. Linda lost a daughter, but Marty? Marty lost his soul.

So, no. No, I didn't think my family would understand if I told them I needed to live as a man. It wasn't going to happen.

❧～❧

KRISTA RETURNED TO COLLEGE WHEN the summer was over, and we stayed in touch through texts and phone calls. One afternoon, I was home with a high fever, so I gave Krista a call on FaceTime.

We were still chatting when Joanna came home from work for a lunch break. "Hey, Joanna, come on over and say hi—it's Krista," I said, inviting her into the conversation.

"Have you been talking to her?" Joanna demanded as soon as I disconnected.

"Yeah, sure," I said. "We keep in touch. Why not?"

"You can't talk to her," Joanna insisted.

But I need this friendship, my thoughts screamed. *Without this friendship I am suicidal!* Something fundamental shifted in this realization, as the idea of another lost friendship seared through me. I could not lose another friend. And that conviction morphed quickly into a resolve: something had to change. Everything had to change. Dr. H had been right. The mental toll was more than I could possibly bear. Thoughts of suicide had increasingly eclipsed my trademark resilience. My survival depended on risking everything I thought I couldn't live without. I just needed some help, some support.

I didn't know how to begin taking risks. I'd spent my whole life pleasing first my family and then Joanna. I didn't know how to advocate for myself. But if I was ever going to figure out how to take big risks, I had to start with small ones. And that's how I ended up across a table at Panera one evening, telling my story—my whole story—to a woman named Cynthia and her husband, Brad.

Cynthia

12

Visitation

THE BURLAP SACKS STOOD IN clusters on the side of the gravel road, a spindly stick protruding from each bundle. Fruit trees, we'd been told.

Ken crouched next to a clump of burlap bags, reaching for one of the sticks. "Mango?"

"I don't know, Ken. I still don't think they need trees. Look around—fruit trees everywhere!"

"It's not about the trees." He shook his head and chuckled in a tone I interpreted as pity. "It's about relationships."

I'd already had this conversation with Ken—the American team leader from the organization our university was traveling with—so I knew what was coming: something about getting out in the community, making friends. Which was fine. What I wasn't sold on was the ulterior motive: foisting ourselves on people so we could ask about their problems and then bow our heads in prayerful supplication on the spot. It was awkward—intrusive.

Ken was unmoved, and there was no getting out of the tree distribution, no chance of being reassigned to the kitchen, to the garden, the library— anywhere there might be a better chance of meeting people in the community and allowing natural, authentic connections to form.

I threw back the last of my coffee—a dark, hand-ground brew as uniquely Haitian as the locals who pan-roasted the raw beans in fresh cane sugar—and joined my son, Brandon, and our university's student-life director, Allie. We walked down the gravel road with several Haitians from the local church our university had partnered with.

I pictured a team of strangers showing up at my door back in Virginia offering random vegetation and light chitchat as a gateway to impromptu prayer, and I just wasn't convinced we had a solid plan for a relationship icebreaker. It seemed exactly the type of do-gooding I'd seen from well-meaning church people every time I'd been to Haiti. I hadn't been immune to it myself on my first trip a few years prior.

I fell hard for Haiti on that visit. Minutes after our turbo prop plane touched down on an expanse of brown soil, I was bumping down a winding dirt road in the back of a military-grade truck and burst into laughter. No one had been happy I'd gone, that first summer. People reminded me that I was taking my son to the most impoverished place in the western hemisphere, a place steeped in voodoo, disease, and danger. But as I took in vivid fuchsia flowers, fabrics on wash lines, faces turning upward as we rolled past, something grabbed me: it was love at first sight. I was hopelessly smitten.

I watched the Haitians watch us as we lumbered by in a billowy haze of dust. I knew they called us the *blancs*: the whites, but they loved us, right? We were here with tools, supplies, and open arms. We had resources, solutions. We were here to help.

An hour later my son and I were in a large, airy room with bunk beds, cribs, and toys, shoulder deep in toddlers—shrieking, giggling toddlers welcoming us to the orphanage they called home. An orphanage we were there to help expand. Somewhere in a tangle of hugs and a game of tag, I became a cliché: a white woman who wanted to take a baby home. What would it take, I wondered, to pluck one of these tots from this orphanage and take them into my family—my white, American, middle-class family? When I casually asked about the adoption process, the answer came as a smackdown to my assumption that giving these kids a "better life" in America was even a goal.

"Oh, no," one of the Haitian orphanage mothers said. "This is their home. We're here to love them and teach them how to become good Haitians."

Oh.

From that moment on, assumptions fell like dominos. I was surrounded by beauty, but also hard truths. I began to question everything—even the way we packed. At our informational session we'd been told to bring clothes we didn't care about—not just because we'd be working but because we should consider leaving everything behind—even our suitcases if we could manage it. Our castoffs were billed as valuable resources. Leaving our sweaty work clothes behind represented even more good we could do on our trip. While every scrap of clothing left on Haitian soil is worn and appreciated, I know now it is a problematic truth. Once Americans began treating Haiti as a dumping ground for used, misprinted, surplus clothes, the Haitian clothing industry buckled—resigning a country of people to wardrobes touting slogans they can't read, products they don't have, and events neither they nor anyone else had ever been to. Bach Week 2010, anyone?

And then there's the matter of "generous" gifts. On the orphanage expansion building site some American team members noticed a group of Haitian men beginning day three of moving a pile of dirt with buckets.

"What do you guys think it would take to purchase a bulldozer for the mission?" one of the men in our group said. Several guys started talking money and availability when someone from the mission spoke up.

"No. Bad idea. Do you know how the community would see a bulldozer?"

The men's eyes narrowed in confusion.

"Lost jobs." I listened as the American with a Haitian address delivered another smackdown. "Those men over there have earned three days' wages thanks to that dirt pile. We can't tamper with their economy. And something goes wrong with the bulldozer? Where would they get it fixed?"

Oh.

And then, in perhaps the most damning indictment of all Christian proselytizing efforts, I met Haitians who traveled on a mission trip of their own to America—because they saw us as spiritually impoverished.

I didn't know it then, on my first trip, but I was there more to be helped than to help. Washing off the first layer of workday grime in the turquoise water every afternoon, holding tiny Black hands, sipping fresh-squeezed juice that tasted of heaven—I romanticized Haiti. So much that I returned four more times with my son, traveling all over a country I adored. I was happy to be a part of some activities that seemed like true partnerships between Haitians and Americans, and, along the way, I thought I had become pretty adept at spotting ill-informed and misguided attempts at well-doing. Now, this prayer pop-in with the stick trees seemed like another attempt to awkwardly insert ourselves into the lives of people we hadn't taken the time to fully understand.

So we proceeded to interrupt a family doing dishes in their outdoor kitchen. We talked with a couple old men who seemed pleased to have the company. And then we arrived at the home of a young woman. She was sitting on her earthen floor doing some sort of chore, perhaps peeling vegetables. Someone introduced her as the wife of someone or other in the Haitian church. She politely accepted the tree, but there was a look around her eyes, a certain weariness.

Someone asked how they could pray for her, and she paused for a moment before answering in Creole. Our interpreter turned to us. "She would like you all to pray that she could somehow start to like going to church."

Had I still been drinking my hand-ground coffee, I would have spewed it mid-swallow. It was all I could do to keep a straight face. Church was something you took in because it was good for you, like V8 or collard greens. Church wasn't meant to be *liked*. Sure, there were people who pretended to enjoy church, much in the way one feigns enjoyment of opera or dense classics—but truly liking church, week in and week out, in perpetuity? It just didn't happen.

"Good luck," I murmured under my breath. Brandon and I exchanged glances. I bit my lip and bowed my head.

It was that moment I realized the visit wasn't just another example of do-gooding Americans getting it wrong—it was *her* church that had sent us to her specifically. This wasn't another half-baked American initiative: this was church being church as I had always known it. Even Haiti wasn't immune to doing dumb things in the name of ministry. The hard truth was we'd been sent here on visitation.

I remembered visitation from my childhood churches, some of which reserved a whole evening every week for sending Bible-toting squads to the homes of people in need of "encouragement." Sometimes they came bearing cookies or random flora; most of the time they had nothing to offer but judgment. Being the subject of visitation was invariably bad. One was at risk of visitation for a wide range of reasons: spotty attendance, rumored bad habits, and suspect doctrine were common. My own family was once the target of a church visitation effort, but I was too young to spot the signs.

I remembered the day well. One spring evening when I was about nine, my mother bolted from the kitchen table and told us to hide. My little sister, Emmie, and I scrambled up the stairs to our bedrooms—two large, adjoined rooms that comprised the entirety of our home's second floor. I slid under my bed, but my window, six inches from the floor, afforded me full view of the street and front yard. I saw a couple of older folks from church exit their car and amble down the front walk. I identified a portly woman who had once announced that she had no sense of smell—making her, in my mind, something akin to a sideshow curiosity. I imagine she was with her husband, and perhaps another person, but these are details I've since dismissed.

We were called out of hiding moments later. Mom looked as if she'd sent a squadron of enemy troops into retreat, but when we asked her why we were hiding from the church people, she was evasive. "Oh, I just didn't want visitors with your father away," she said, attempting to shoo off the discussion. Our father was on a two-week trip to Singapore with the Gideons, the organization behind every Bible currently resting in a hotel nightstand.

My mother may have won the battle, but the persistence of the church people was not to be underestimated. They would return a few days later, and she would let them in. It wasn't until my father was back in our kitchen that I learned the reason for the visit.

"Who does such a thing?" he fumed, pounding a fist on the table. "Who makes a special trip to someone's house just to say they *aren't* praying for them?" It seemed the church leaders came by to explain that my father's wanton distribution of scripture was not condoned. His time, effort, and money needed to be filtered through their approval, their leadership. His trip with the Gideons was in flagrant disregard of their counsel, and they wanted to send a clear message: their prayers were not with him in Singapore, or with my mother on the home front. Our family was operating in a void of prayer support, and my mother needed to know.

ALTHOUGH IT WOULD BE ACCURATE to say that I grew up in the church, the singular here implies a neatly constructed unity that doesn't remotely describe my experience going to churches, plural. My childhood was a veritable kaleidoscope of religious expression. I was eight years old when my father—an alumnus of 1960s-era peace and love and dabbler in 1970s Transcendental Meditation—discovered Christianity during a televised Billy Graham crusade. From the moment he turned the dial of the black-and-white, rabbit-eared TV to the off position, I became well versed in multiple approaches to scripture: Methodist, Bible, Bible Baptist, Charismatic, Presbyterian, Plain-Old Baptist. Most protestant thought would enjoy a period of veneration in our home—but never Catholicism, which was verboten for reasons that were never clear. No matter what church we attended, a pendulum of faith regulated our daily activities and decisions. The weight bobbed rhythmically back and forth for varying periods before taking wild and often erratic swings from the left to the right on either individual topics or entire denominational platforms.

The first church I really remember was a little clapboard affair in the hills of the New York Southern Tier, where we moved after my father became disillusioned with his mercurial career in commercial radio and abandoned a lucrative contract with a station in Cleveland, Ohio, to join my grandparents at the family spinning mill. My parents, George, an Italian American with balding curly hair and dark-rimmed glasses, and Margaret, a tall, mild-mannered blonde with long, pin-straight hair, bought a crumbling farmhouse at the intersection of a narrow gravel road and paved street. The wider road serviced downward of ten vehicles per day, mostly RVs en route to a nearby campground. Traffic on the gravel road was regarded with curiosity that boarded on suspicion. My parents were deep in a Thoreau-esque quest for authentic experience, in search of the kind of bounty that city life couldn't offer: a garden, fresh-baked pies plump with wild berries, forts and tree swings. Enter Billy Graham, a handful of starter churches, and then the little congregation of farmers who filed into polished pews at the Locust Hill Bible Church each week to sing from hardbound hymnals with threadbare covers.

I can still travel the route in my mind: an ascent up the dirt road across from the house, a right-hand turn onto another dirt road midway up the hill, some twists and bends, and the simple white building nestled amid verdant cow pastures. In truth, if I were to find myself suddenly at the wheel on one of these gravel roads, it's unlikely that I could actually find the church, if it even still exists. My mind has smoothed over the particulars of the path—simplified the nuances, edited some of the forks. I've lost key details that give true access to the place, making its existence a function of my memory. Sometimes I almost smell it more than I can see it—outside, a wonderful dewy aroma, the stuff of grasses and wildflowers and rocky creek beds; the interior a mixture of must and dust and old wood that seeped from the marrow of the building, amplifying itself in the un-air-conditioned heat of summer.

The church became our community, our home base. Sunday services and Wednesday prayer meetings were weekly touchstones—safe and familiar. Church life was an extension of family life and mirrored it in many ways. For one thing, there were chores. One Saturday afternoon each month, we piled into the family car for our turn cleaning the church building. My mom would head to the kitchen, Dad would navigate a vacuum or lawnmower, and I'd head to the sanctuary to dust the hardwood pews while Emmie played. There's no chance I was a thorough duster, as most of my memories in the empty sanctuary are of running up and down the aisles or taking in the view from behind the pulpit—things I wasn't allowed to do when adults were present.

But church wasn't all work—it was where you found your friends. Pastor Blessing and his wife were just a bit older than my parents, maybe thirty, and their daughters, Juliana and Sadie—brown-eyed girls with curly brown hair—were about my age. Since my family was almost as involved in church life as the pastor's clan, our families became fast friends. Dinner at each other's homes would invariably end with three voices begging for permission to sleep over, a plea that enjoyed a variable success rate.

But this simple time in the little country church ended in scandal when Pastor Blessing and his family began speaking in tongues, a practice that involved the involuntary utterance of unknown languages. Although the story about "tongues of fire" being conferred on early Christians came straight from Acts chapter two in the Bible, I heard adults describe the practice as "not for today" in a tone that conveyed that dabbling in the "dark art" of tongues represented more than a spiritual quirk, but, rather, crossing a line of demarcation.

Even as a child, I instinctively understood the power of lines. I hadn't yet learned the vocabulary I'd use later as an elementary art teacher to describe *unity*—the art principle that allows diverse textures, colors, and materials to become a harmonious, cohesive whole—but I knew something of lines. In art class—my favorite—lines marked the places we colored inside. The boxy houses I drew, the dot-to-dot patterns I connected in activity books, the concentric patterns that flowed from the pens in my Spirograph set—all lines. I also knew lines as boundaries—my father's finger drawing invisible fences around our property, indicating the separation between protection and the unknown, where I belonged and where I didn't. Lines told stories: where things began, where they ended, what was included, and what wasn't. And if there was anything I liked better than art, it was a story.

But this story, of why I could no longer play with Juliana and Sadie, why we'd never again drive those twisty roads to sit in those hard, polished pews, seemed disconnected with the lessons of love I learned inside those walls. This story was my first glimpse into what happened when someone ventured beyond established boundaries and into the space outside the lines.

Lesson: communities cannot disagree.

Soon we were attending a new, bigger church with more opportunities. My sister and I joined Awana, a kind of spiritual scouting program. There were vests, patches, handbooks, and ranks to work through, and I tackled it all like it was my life's work. And in a way, I suppose it was. To this day I attribute most of my Bible knowledge to my efforts to earn scripture memory badges during weekly club meetings. In Awana, right answers were a currency that garnered applause and awards. As a gangly, bookish kid on the periphery of the elementary school social scene, I craved the accolades, accumulating "Clubber of the Month" ribbons with a consistency that rivaled the calendar itself.

My Awana leaders held the status of mini celebrities in my life. I remember phone calls and sledding parties—things that let me know I was more to them than a weekly duty. Likewise, club for me was a lifestyle rather than an event. My church connections and projects kept me grounded and focused; they gave me a sense of purpose.

Our family settled in at the Bible Baptist church for some time. I worked my way through several Awana ranks, and my dad took over the teen boys' Sunday school class. Our house became a second home for some of the boys, giving Emmie and me a cadre of surrogate brothers. Church provided a nurturing foundation for my childhood. This was good for me, but in no way indicative of the Bible Baptist church serving as an inclusive community for just anyone in need of an anchor.

I would hear rumblings of incidents that rankled my parents' sense of justice: the young newcomer who was asked to leave because he'd entered the sanctuary with a guitar, my father's dwindling favor with church leadership for befriending a local mink farmer who'd been marginalized for mysterious infractions, and their general disapproval of my father's involvement with the Gideons. I was eleven when we left the Bible Baptist church. I don't recall why, but I do remember the event that signaled the next major swing of our pendulum of faith. Late one night, I tiptoed into the kitchen for a drink and found my father leaning against the tall coal furnace in the back of the room, head bowed, hands clasped, fervently muttering incomprehensible phrases. I paused for a moment, listening to be sure. *Tongues!* I quietly retreated back upstairs, deciding to remain silent and await further developments.

Eliminating the concept that tongues was a great evil seemed to expand my world. My father had crossed the same line Pastor Blessing had years earlier, and here we were on the other side of that breached boundary. And nothing had shattered. In fact, things seemed more complete. The shift signaled the return of the Blessing family, with whom we began enjoying meals and friendship once again. New people with kids my age began coming to the house. Sometimes we even went to Charismatic church, where everyone spoke in tongues. Since a lot seemed to ride socially on this mysterious practice—or gift, as my new friends called it—I wanted to see for myself what the fuss was about.

"It's a prayer language," Juliana said one evening as we sat on the floor in my room next to my large wooden toy box, play paused somewhere between Barbies and my Jewel Magic jewelry maker. "It's a gift from God that helps you pray better because you are speaking God's own language."

God's own language! How exciting! I wanted in. "How do you do it?" I asked. Everyone seemed to automatically know how this thing worked, and I remained clueless.

"You pray that God will give it to you," Juliana said. "Here, let me show you." We dropped the lid of the toy box and Juliana rested her elbows on the surface. She clamped her eyes shut and remained still and silent for a moment, her brown curls framing her face in cherubic rings. She then began repeating a rhythmic phrase, quietly at first, and then in earnest. She opened her eyes. "Now I'll pray for you to receive the gift."

I squeezed my eyes closed just as I'd seen Juliana do moments earlier. I sat in silence while she prayed for me. I waited. Nothing.

"Maybe you need to get a pastor to pray for you," Juliana said.

So next time I went to Charismatic church, I crept down the aisle and asked the pastor to lay hands on me. He petitioned the Lord with fervor on my behalf for several minutes before encouraging me to "say whatever came to mind." At one point, I mumbled some convincing syllables, but I felt silly, fraudulent, and warm with shame. If the gift of tongues was a thing, I wasn't getting it. But I wasn't alone. My mother didn't like Charismatic church and didn't get the gift either. Our trips to Charismatic church became less frequent, and eventually stopped altogether. The Blessings and our new friends faded from our lives.

Lesson: people leave if you disagree.

Our next church was a small Presbyterian congregation that met in an old, white church with tall stained-glass windows and a working bell tower. It was situated on the main street of a neighboring town, and it was the setting for my entire early-teen world. The pastor, Reverend Carson, was a gentle, soft-spoken man who devoted hours each week to the youth. He met with us in the church's upper room on Sunday mornings and around a bottomless bowl of popcorn in his living room Sunday nights. If a Christian band was playing within a couple hours' drive, he would take a group—even on weeknights. He'd personally facilitate and often fund just about any idea we'd imagine. We turned the fellowship hall into a haunted house on Halloween and held countless fundraisers—car washes, hoagie sales, bake auctions—for trips: good ones to the nation's capital and multi-day music festivals.

Reverend Carson's Christianity seemed to draw lines of connection rather than boundary—inclusion as opposed to exclusion. His spirituality included cross-faith dialogue, social justice, and activism. The secular and the sacred, the political and the spiritual weren't separate spheres, but dual aspects of a larger whole. Even though as a young teen I was more interested in youth group for the social opportunities than spiritual ones, I recognized something different in Reverend Carson's brand of church, and I liked it. A lot. But a border line still divided my construct of faith, making it impossible for me to see a cohesive picture.

This unencumbered time in my personal church history corresponded with what I'd come to regard as my father's conservative period. Perhaps to counterbalance the more liberal mindset that prevailed at church, he adopted stringent standards at home, particularly in terms of what we were allowed to watch and listen to. He occasionally objected even to movies that Reverend Carson took us to see, such as the 1982 blockbuster *Gandhi*, whom Reverend Carson viewed as a role model and my father considered a cult leader. My grandmother began smuggling VHS tapes of recorded shows for us to watch when our parents were at work. I frequently felt guilty for thriving at church but covertly gorging on contraband at home. A boundary still existed—this time between home standards of Christianity and the more interesting version Reverend Carson's faith seemed to offer. The two often coincided, but not enough to assuage a gnawing sense of conflict.

Lesson: I don't agree with people I care about—and that is dangerous.

My time at the Presbyterian church was cut tragically short when my father and grandfather were forced to shutter the family spinning mill—the source of livelihood that had made it possible for him to walk away from radio years earlier. He decided to return to broadcasting, but this time at a Christian radio station hours away from the farmhouse that, thanks to almost a decade of toil, was a snug and charming home. After the move my father was contractually obligated to attend the nondescript, straitlaced, fundamental Baptist church whose Sunday service aired live on the station. His faith explorations continued, but they became less obvious, more personal, and restricted to issues he explored between the covers of countless books and wrestled within the arena of his own mind.

My own spiritual investigation, though, was just beginning. I had to figure out what to make of the broad range of revolving perspectives I'd experienced. On one hand, it was impossible not to see the conditional nature of church communities, and the lessons I absorbed remained with me. I simply couldn't miss the message that inclusion depended on conformity. Someone can be a cherished member of an all-consuming "family" one Sunday and excommunicated the next. But in a way, observing shoddy Christianity ultimately managed to do more to strengthen my faith than squelch it. Being raised by someone who explored everything so as not to miss anything gave me a sense of the many varied and valid ways to approach faith. In fact, my idea of God kept getting bigger with each failed attempt I saw to contain him.

It was against this checkered backdrop that I evaluated my adult experiences with organized Christianity—including the tree distribution that second trip to Haiti. I'll never know the backstory of why the young Haitian woman was targeted for visitation, the details of how her less-than-enthusiastic regard for church may have manifested and registered with her community. Perhaps the whole visit was really just a friendly tree delivery: Teleflora, Haitian style. Maybe she broached the topic of her lack of ardor for collective worship because it was genuinely on her mind. Who knows? Regardless, I would love to have another ten minutes and the Creole skills to have a real conversation with her, minus the interpreter. I'd pop a squat beside her on the earthen floor, grab a vegetable from the peeling pile, and say, "You know what? Chances are, you're never going to like church, and that's okay. I'm not sure God likes church much either, and that means you just might have a better chance finding him out here than in there."

But those fleeting moments I did have in her home came at an awkward middle ground in my spiritual journey: before Danny, before the Inlet, before the unexpected tenure-track promotion, before my spiritual life and then my inner world burned to the ground—yet long after I took my turn at being part of the problem.

13

Party Lines

THE PROBLEM WITH ME WAS that I wasn't always as skeptical of church as I was on that hot weekday morning in Haiti. When my husband, Brad, and I married at twenty-one, there was no question we'd be church people. It was how we were raised. It was all we knew. Looking back, I realize we barely knew ourselves as individuals then, let alone as a unit. I had vague notions of becoming a writer, professor, or artist, while Brad was finding his way into a career in IT. We were still figuring ourselves out. But church was a no-brainer. We drew on our growing-up experiences to square ourselves roughly within the world of mainstream, GOP, evangelical Christianity, even though we hadn't settled on a particular substrain. We would figure it out—find a congregation and invest our entire lives in it.

One Sunday evening we were standing just inside the door of our newly adopted church, still trying to figure out our role in both the congregation and the larger faith community. We had recently moved to Virginia and found our way to a small, round church that managed to simultaneously simulate the most awkward and awesome elements of a family reunion every time the doors opened. We had the overly friendly uncle soaked in old-man aftershave, a gaggle of free-range children, and a squadron of grandmothers permanently stationed in the kitchen. While my husband and I may not have agreed with either each other or the church on every point of spiritual contention, the after-service cookies, warbly hymns, and makeshift programming—no vests or badges here—gave the place a heartwarming, homespun vibe that appealed to us as a young couple settling down in a new state.

Hovering inside the door that evening, we must have looked every bit the seekers we were, because one of the church moms approached us. "You guys need to go help out with our teens," she said. "They could use some fresh young faces in there." Brad and I locked eyes. Hanging with teenagers sounded better than sitting in the main sanctuary. Suddenly we were youth group leaders.

A life of late-night movies, floors littered with dishes and sleeping bodies, and the occasional 2:00 a.m. phone call alerting us to a forgotten aerosol can of deodorant in the oven is not for everyone. In fact, it's probably for hardly anyone—but Brad and I loved having what often seemed like a Duggar-esque number of younger siblings. Bonus: we had a bottomless list of potential babysitters for our toddler, Allison, and infant son, Brandon.

My blond-haired, blue-eyed husband exuded a quiet confidence to which the teens gravitated. I was louder, bolder, and more apt to involve us in adventure, calamity, or some combination of the two. We were a well-balanced team. It was a good role for us.

But it was a role we almost had to vacate before it truly got off the ground. Months into our adoption of overnight lock-ins, pizza parties, and Sunday Bible studies as a lifestyle, the minister of the round church requested to come to our house for a chat. I was old enough now to know that we were the subjects of a visitation effort. I also knew why.

The round church had very specific ideas about baptism. Heaven-and-hell-level ideas. It wasn't enough to just *get* baptized—you also had to believe that the Holy Spirit entered your heart and saved your soul at the exact moment you came up from the water. If you were to perish, for instance, en route to a baptismal fount, then God help you. We trust the Lord is merciful. Their belief about the power of baptism was both shockingly literal and ridiculously important to them. I don't want to think anyone's eternal fate is tied to a split-second dunk in the water—a technicality. Technicalities are the worst kind of lines: barriers. I was fine with the idea of getting baptized, and, honestly, the issue seemed moot as long as one just went ahead and—ahem—took the plunge. The magic would happen when it happened, even though I doubted that magic was at play at all. Baptism seemed more to me like a public statement, a symbol—something metaphorically helpful.

It soon became clear that this issue of baptism was like the issue of tongues reincarnated. It was another line of demarcation separating the spiritually sound from the heretics. It didn't take long for the church leadership to discover that Brad and I did not regard baptism with the level of mystic importance required of their leaders. Thus, the visit from the pastor. I knew this interaction would determine our future with the youth. I worried that our relationship with them would be severed because we couldn't confidently pinpoint the exact moment a soul was saved from hellfire. But the relationships we were forming with our teens were a salvation in the here and now for Brad and me, and, it seemed, for them too. I was determined to avoid an ouster.

The day of the visit, I put extra effort into cleaning. I made sure I had baked goods on hand. But most of all, I worked phrases over in my mind, attempting to be both genuine and conforming, open yet committed. I was looking for verbal sleights of hand that would allow us room to hold our personal opinions yet fully support the mission of the church. But honestly? I wanted this version of family so badly I was prepared to find a way to adopt their perspective. I'd will myself to reimagine the clutch role of baptism if it meant being able to stay in this community with my teens.

If the round church was a family, the minister was a mealy, nervous second cousin who had to be included despite having little to add to the festivities. Our visit with him wasn't memorable in any way, but I do recall it leading to some kind of follow-up meeting around a Sunday school table. I don't remember what exactly we said, but I know we were somehow deemed worthy to serve, which we did with wholehearted investment. In time we became part of the fabric of the community. The milquetoast minister moved on shortly after his visit with us and was replaced by Scott, a laid-back, jovial family man.

By the time Scott arrived, we were so deeply embedded in the inner workings of the church that Brad was among the leaders who vetted Scott before he was hired. We were running in the inner circle—that safe, protected place inside the boundary lines—and I loved it. I had somewhere I belonged. I was surrounded by people who cared about me, doted on my babies, invited us to … everything. When we weren't hosting lock-ins or movie nights with the teens, we were at a meeting, a potluck, or just hanging out with all the friends we now had. Being inside the lines often means you are part of a well-composed canvas—living in a gallery-wrapped, frame-ready, picture-perfect life.

One weekend, my parents were visiting and joined us for Sunday services. We entered that same door where we'd stood just a couple years earlier when we were new and unsure—but now, every time we passed through the entrance, we walked straight into the very literal open arms of our friends and community. That day at least half a dozen people approached me for an opinion, idea, or just a hug before we even left the entrance. Later my mom observed, "You're really important to your church," and I basked in the realization of this truth. I belonged there. That was my space. Those were my people. And my work there mattered, for eternity. It was so simple, so clear. Life made sense; I had so many answers, and I was so very sure.

AFTER SIX YEARS AT THE round church, Brad and I found ourselves in a drab room on the first floor of a Baptist church along the beachfront near our house. Situated at the end of a poorly lit hallway, the long-forgotten room had been offered to Brad and me as a youth office at the new post we'd accepted at the struggling church. This new position wasn't volunteer work: we were part-time paid staff, hired in hopes of salvaging a lagging youth program.

Brad and I were either taking our leave from the round church or on an extended hiatus, depending on which one of us you asked when. The prevailing family atmosphere had skewed toward the dysfunctional in the months prior to our departure. We'd been to several meetings that felt more like family court than fellowship. One Sunday I paused by the bulletin board on the wall by the main door and saw the printed minutes of a contentious board meeting Brad attended—a meeting during which, the record showed, he'd called the rest of the group "slackers." Six times. You know the feeling when someone prints out a transcript of your last big family feud and posts it by the front door next to the rustic *Live, Laugh, Love* sign and below the framed family photo? No? Well, it was kind of like that. It was definitely time for a break.

We came to the Baptist church in the aftermath of some sort of shake-up that had taken their beloved pastor and equally revered youth leader as causalities. Instability and tenuous trust colored most of our interactions with the parishioners, who vacillated between giving us free rein to revamp the program and questioning our every decision. We were neither Baptist nor interested in becoming Baptist, which, for them, was tantamount to a gamble in already shaky times.

We'd ultimately been hired after winning over a committee of church members who grilled us over several sessions around a boardroom table. At one point, an older parishioner asked me a question about my life goals, and suddenly I was describing my latent vison of becoming a professor "when I grew up"—the kind with a bustling office and students crowded around an enormous table at some old, sprawling house. My beloved professor alter ego, conceived from the DNA of forgotten films and assorted literature, seemed to charm this man, who seemed delighted by the idea that I was still anticipating another, different sort of life in the future. His eyes twinkled as he slapped his thigh. "When I grow up!" he repeated. "I love that!" Although he was laughing, it was obvious he took me seriously, even though he would have had every reason for skepticism. I was newly thirty with nothing but a bachelor's degree and no plans or means to return to school. Yet I somehow sensed this other life would find me, that it was meant to be. But at that time, other students in a different venue—that threadbare Baptist church—needed my focus and attention. We were eager to win over those who doubted us and, more importantly, send the teens some swift signals that we were invested—that they were safe.

I wanted to transform the forgotten office into one of those signals. One look at the cheap, dark paneling and sickly blue built-in bookcase sent me running to the Home Depot. I returned with paint cans and brushes, slathering coats of sunny yellow over the dark paneling. I painted the rectangular sections of the bookcase blue, green, and Creamsicle orange and tossed around some large throw pillows, a beanbag or two, and an oversized inflatable chair. Instant hangout. Even though the youth group had been given the run of the building's entire third floor, I saw the office space as the inner sanctum—safe, cozy, comfortable. A place to open up, to be heard.

I remembered the difference Reverend Carson made in my life during my teen years, and I wanted to replicate the sense of possibility and adventure he modeled for what a youth group—and a safe space—could become. Eventually resource books and drama scripts spilled from the shelves and posters from events we attended turned the walls into a group scrapbook. I know, intellectually, that people came and laughed and bonds were forged, but as far as heart-to-heart conversations, the only specific talk I remember in that space is the one that still haunts me.

One Wednesday evening, Steve, one of our core students, popped his head in the office door. He was early—well ahead of our group meeting time. This wasn't unusual for Steve, who rode his bike or walked from his home in one of the tumbledown shacks—billed collectively and optimistically as "cottages"—clustered in the block between the church and the Chesapeake Bay. Steve was not just a regular attender; he was more like a constant presence. His voice was thin, his build gangly, and he clung to church like a lifeline. Group simply didn't happen without Steve.

That evening he had something on his mind. "Can we talk for a minute?" His voice shook as he sank into the orange inflatable chair.

I left my desk and settled into some combination of pillows and beanbag near the door. "What's up, Steve?"

I don't remember his lead-up, but his ending jolted me to attention. "I'm gay," he said, stealing a glance at me before returning his gaze to his fidgeting hands.

My stomach flip-flopped and my hands felt clammy. Although my husband and I hung out around the borderlands of mainstream evangelical Christianity, we were still part of the population—leaders, even. There was still right and there was still wrong, and on this issue, middle ground was not an option. This was an answer I knew. Homosexuality was wrong. There was no question what I'd say. I knew what the situation demanded. I just wasn't sure I could say it, there, then, to his face.

Everything about that moment felt heavy: Steve, sinking into the inflatable chair, the pit in my stomach—even the air. I am sure I fumbled through some basic acknowledgment of his story, but the only thing I remember saying is, "The Bible calls it sin."

Steve's lips pressed into a flat line. He nodded slowly, not bothering to bring his head back up once his eyes returned to his lap.

When he finally looked up, his face was set. He managed a smile. "Thank you," he said, as he stood up and headed out the door and up the stairs to group. And that was it; we never spoke of it again.

I wanted something more to say, but my role seemed clear. As Steve's youth leader it was my job to steer him away from sin and bad choices. Because, to my 1990s conservative Christian sensibilities, that's what we were dealing with here: the poor choice of a kid who needed better role models. The mission, then, was to definitively label Steve's sexuality as sin yet somehow keep him coming to group—the source, I was sure, of the love and encouragement that would replace his desire for guys. I rushed to assure him that we still loved him and that he was a valued member of the group. To his credit, Steve kept coming. He kept engaging. He continued messaging me throughout the week with comments about bands we liked and ideas about youth group plans. He just knew what to keep quiet.

But yet . . . something was wrong, and I knew it. I'd drawn a boundary line and put Steve on the outside, stranded, with no path back beyond becoming someone he wasn't. Not even Reverend Carson, with his bottomless bowls of popcorn, liberal politics, and inclusive attitude had given me a model for navigating this relationship; LGBTQIA+ issues simply never came up. I knew I gave Steve the right answer, but that didn't keep a nagging discomfort from settling deep inside me.

Months after my conversation with Steve, our group went on a joint trip to a music festival with the teens from the round church. Scott, our former pastor at the round church, was curious about Steve. "Is he gay?" Scott asked me one day as we were walking to our campsite.

"Yes," I said.

"Does he have a strong relationship with his father?"

"No, he lives with his mom. No dad in the picture."

Scott nodded. "It's been my experience that effeminate boys lack strong male role models."

That was always the conversation about anyone outside the conventional norms so strongly guarded in the church: What was wrong? What could we fix? But in my continued interactions with Steve, I didn't sense that anything *was* particularly wrong with the kid who devoted his time, energies, and efforts exclusively to whatever was going on inside church doors. He was loyal, passionate, kind. I was increasingly confident that there were missing pieces in the narrative I'd been given. Something akin to a quest began to shape itself in my mind. I wanted the rest of the story.

So I began what became a years-long process of clicking around the still-new internet, learning what I could. I sought out, read, and absorbed the painful experiences of kids like Steve—people who loved the church but also had same-sex crushes. I'd like to say that after immersing myself in their world and realities, I never again walked away from the story of a confused and hurting person at the intersection of gender, sexuality, and faith, but that wouldn't be entirely accurate.

At the time, I was collaborating with the youth group girls on a writing project: a young adult novel about a group of counselors at a fictional summer camp. The teens populating my fictional camp were plagued by the same gamut of issues and insecurities as the actual teens in my life, and several of the girls were working with me on the plotline. We had a book club of sorts, only with a story we were writing, rather than reading.

Kristin, one of the fictional camp counselors, may have been a fabrication of my imagination, but I still carry a fair amount of guilt for abandoning her cause. A seventeen-year-old with long blonde hair and a Southern drawl, she foisted herself into the story—and my life—the same way any fictional character ever has: as a fully developed individual—as real to me as the people I see face-to-face. When I write fiction, typically the deal is, characters show up and I document their stories. A sure sign of a good fiction-writing day is when I am surprised by what happens—when I've gotten so deep into the story that I am simply a conduit. Since I seem to do my best work when I allow my characters to do the heavy lifting, I try to stay out of the way and let them tell their stories. It has been this way with every character I've written about—except Kristin.

Despite her classic, cheerleader good looks, I knew the Kristin character wasn't comfortable in her own skin. Every plotline in which she appeared left her at odds with the female counselors, particularly when the subject turned to dating. The reason was not a mystery to me: I knew that the Kristin character was, at a minimum, questioning, if not a lesbian. I wanted to write her story—I knew it was important. I knew exploring her narrative would not only help me find some better answers; it had the potential to spark dialogue with future readers. As a creative person, I work things out artistically: in print, paint, or other malleable medium. Art offers tough subjects a plasticity that I find missing in the rest of my life. Nuanced plotlines, softened edges, blended borders, contrast, perspective, and depth give me a language to make sense of complexity in life, a platform to explore the many shades a fully realized picture requires.

My online quest was teaching me that not only in my youth group, but in the church at large, topics around gender and sexuality could no longer be ignored. I wanted to help start the conversation. I saw the Kristin character as a creative echo of real-life narratives that were increasingly bouncing off the walls of my church office and my living room. Time would reveal that Steve wasn't the only gay student in our group. Over the eighteen months we were in the position, we would discover that at least a quarter of our core members had same-sex attractions. These were high-stakes coming-of-age stories that were all but forbidden to discuss in the better churches of the early millennium. I dreamed of writing a story that included the fictional Kristin's (and, by extension, our real-life youths') struggles. But I bailed. I couldn't see my way past the absurdity of presenting a queer character to the Christians I saw as the market for my book. I'd be branded; the counselors and I would be blackballed. So I wrote Kristin into a relationship with a male counselor and convinced myself that the original plotline had been, if not a whim, a very bad idea for someone interested in marketing books to churched teens. In short, I sold Kristin out. Conformity meant acceptance, and I prized above all else having a place to belong.

My desire to be accepted made me a coward, afraid to broach a topic that would get me shunned by the pack, the surety of which was clarified on a sunny spring morning shortly after my book's sequel came out. I was in central Pennsylvania on a visit with family. The trip had morphed into a mini book tour: a couple of bookstore signings, a workshop at my high school alma mater, and other small-town-girl-returns-from-the-big-city events. I was eager to play the role: updating my blog, changing my outfits, thinking up witty one-liners. My father had a colleague in a neighboring town who hosted a live, call-in type show that touted "wide-ranging discussion on issues of the day." Discovering I was in town, the broadcaster—we'll call him Dean—invited me to come on his show. We were going to discuss issues from the book's plot: underage drinking, foreign mission trips, and finding purpose in life. I was also prepared to field questions about my youth work from the conservative, Christian listener base in the small community nestled around the campus of Bucknell University.

I wasn't thinking about Kristen's story that Wednesday morning as I sat with my father in the radio station's lobby. Honestly, I was thinking about the potential for the radio segment to boost attendance at my reading that night.

But as the lobby airwaves filled with the feed from the studio where Dean, a burly, bearded man in his late fifties, was interviewing his first guest, my thoughts quickly turned to my abandoned fictional character. Opening the show that morning was Dr. Paul Cameron, chairman of the Family Research Institute, an operation devoted solely to cranking out studies linking homosexuality to pedophilia and other ills.

Cameron was on the air to share findings from his most recent study suggesting that homosexuals have a life expectancy twenty years lower than the average person, causing the good doctor to fret over the cost of educating them. My dad and I shared a panicked glance as Cameron snorted, "They are not going to live long enough to pay back society. They don't live long enough or work hard enough. They don't hold up their end of the sky." I squirmed, wishing the segment was over, even though it had just begun.

"Don't be gay," Cameron urged parents to tell their children. "Stay away from this kind of activity. It's super bad for you!" his piped-in voice enthused. "You don't want to associate with them, but they want to associate with you." Ideally, Cameron said, gay people would look at their life expectancy statistics and say, "'What I do is so dangerous, I shouldn't subject people to it,' but instead they say, 'I don't care. I want that duplex.'" Cameron's voice cackled in excitement. "You don't want them living next door," he concluded. "They are far more apt to have sex with animals—and our kids!"

My father and I sat in the lobby with our gazes to the floor as the rant in the studio continued. I thought about friends who had been sharing the show's link on social media, encouraging people to tune in to hear me talk about my book. A sick, queasy embarrassment settled in the pit of my stomach as I imagined someone stumbling on the Cameron segment of the broadcast associating me with the bigoted propaganda traversing the airwaves.

At this point, I didn't know that Cameron had run afoul of the American Psychological Association (APA), the American Sociological Association (ASA), and the Canadian Psychological Association or his organization's classification as a hate group by the Southern Poverty Law Center. I hadn't read his interview in Rolling Stone where he stated: "Marital sex tends toward the boring end. Generally, it doesn't deliver the kind of sheer sexual pleasure that homosexual sex does … if all you want is the most satisfying orgasm you can get, then homosexuality seems too powerful to resist."

But Dean, the interviewer, never mentioned the rampant criticisms of Cameron's work or near-admission of his own same-sex attraction. And rather than balancing Cameron's perspective with that of an opposing viewpoint, he simply reminded listeners that Cameron spoke "from empirical evidence." Not only was this sloppy journalism, it was false advertising. Listeners weren't getting far-ranging discussion but dogma and bigotry cloaked as science.

And then it was my turn at the mic. Maybe another version of me would have done better. Maybe today, I'd find a way to turn my segment into a challenge to what had just happened. Maybe a braver me would have been certain to work in mention of our quarter-gay youth group and how having nothing to offer them in terms of advice, resources, or hope had been humbling, scary, and life changing. Maybe I'd talk about suicide rates among LGBTQIA+ teens and the tragedy of a supposedly pro-life church standing idly by. We'll never know what a different version of me would do, because the only version of me that was actually behind the microphone was an absolute disappointment. The person in the studio that day may have been privately outraged by what happened in the room moments earlier, but publicly? No way was she using her platform to do anything risky.

So I talked up my book, cheesed for some photos, shook hands with Dean. On the way out I accepted the CD recording he handed me of the day's show. The whole show. Dr. Paul Cameron's hate-laced bigotry as the preamble to my discussion about teens and the issues that plagued them. At least the teens it was acceptable to speak of—the gay teens would have to do what they always did and suffer in the collective silence.

14

Outliers

I MAY HAVE BEEN DABBLING in dozens of gray-scale tones beyond the church's standard-issue, black-and-white palette, but I still clung to one pretty simplistic principle: I believed in brownies. These humble chocolate squares were powerful bonding agents. Give opposing forces an hour and a table with a pan of warm, moist squares and a pot of coffee, and friends will depart sixty minutes later. I saw it happen all the time on a micro scale, and I suspected that, if tested, brownie mediation would hold up in larger trials.

I admit that I might be giving a tad too much credit to the average brownie. But my brownies? They are magic. To this day these brownies remain legendary among a subset of now-thirtysomething women who made it a practice to meet me around a pan of still-warm, double-chocolate goodness in my living room every Tuesday night throughout their teen years. During these hours each week we laughed, cried, read, discussed, and even argued, the chocolate nucleus holding us together at the core. During seasons when our membership was large, I made double batches in a nine-by-thirteen-inch cake pan. In eras when we could all fit comfortably across my love seat and sofa, we got by with a standard square brownie pan. Ordinary Tuesdays meant cutting a section from your favorite part of the pan—some of us were edge-piece people; for others, only the gooey center would do— and settling in. Birthdays meant going home with an entire brownie bag all to yourself. And then, there were mediation brownies. We may not have called them that in the moment, but that doesn't change the fact that brownies were occasionally deployed in times of crisis.

Our Tuesday group was a sacred community, and I vowed in my heart to invest in every girl who came through my door. And it wasn't hard. I loved these girls—their ideas, their laughter, and their questions. The hours I spent with them gave me life. But the girls did not always have the same type of tried-and-true commitment to each other. Teen communities are often constructed on the instable landscape of doubt, insecurity, competition, and jealousy. The winds shift rapidly over this terrain. But I refused to let shaky allegiances damage the community we created. So any time conflict threatened our borders, we had a system in place. The feuding parties would agree to meet at my coffee table with a pan of brownies—and me—as a buffer.

I said very little at these sessions beyond inviting each girl to share her story and promising to keep the other party from interrupting, even though they seldom did. These sessions would always end with untangled miscommunications and both parties feeling heard. Chocolate, shared stories, laughter, forgiveness—every time. I began to believe that all conflict might be resolved this way: warring factions, lured by tasty feel-good compounds, arriving at a moment of shared humanity. Chocolate and, ideally, coffee were keys; the real power, I knew, was in personal stories.

I still believe this. There's nothing quite as powerful as a personal narrative—the gift of entering another's thoughts, experiences, and reality—to glimpse, ever so briefly, life through a radically different lens. But I have come to realize that I was overlooking the importance of another element at work in those sessions: having someone—in the girls' case, me—say, "I've got you. I won't let this go bad. You are safe, both of you." By degrees I have come to see that all advocacy provides this support structure, this safety net. To advocate for someone is to say, "I am here, I am standing with you: I won't let you go down alone."

Because that's what we're afraid of. We tone down our voices and mute our identities out of fear of the repercussions, the aftermath. That's why it's hard, if not impossible, to do advocacy work for others in the absence of your own safety net. I could advocate for the girls because I was more than ten years their senior. I had a home, a marriage, and years of buffer between their teenage concerns and my reality. My comparative stability allowed me to sit in the middle of their storms without feeling the full impact of their intensity.

The first time I can recall consciously checking to see if I had backup support before amplifying my voice happened after Brad and I returned to the round church. Our stint at the Baptist congregation unraveled after a mere eighteen months, and we decided to reinsert ourselves back into our former congregation, which is how I came to sign on as a chaperone for a week of camp. The round church was part of a group of sister congregations that jointly owned a rustic campground with a few ragtag cabins, a modest multipurpose building, a pool, and acres of woods and fields. In the summer, each church took a turn hosting a week of camp: developing a theme, games, and programming and providing the staff to make it happen.

By that time, I was working as an art teacher and a freelance journalist as well as shuttling my kids to and from school, soccer games, and music lessons. Our lives had shifted, and so had the structure of the round church's youth ministry, which now had a full-time youth minister. We returned to the round church as regular parishioners—involved with the youth, but not in an official capacity. In the summers, I went as a female sponsor on all the youth trips, usually with both kids in tow—Allison as a younger participant and Brandon as well-loved mascot.

And so it was that our newly hired youth minister, Austin, a recent Bible college grad in his early twenties, was put in charge of our church's week at camp. The theme was superheroes, a motif reflected only when Austin or one of his Bible college buddies would don a costume to preach for an hour every evening. Otherwise, chaos reigned. We had regular meals and pool time, but by every other measure, camp that week resembled a low-rent boys' club. Austin and his pals hung out in an air-conditioned office eating popsicles and playing video games, emerging at points to hop into a pickup game, jump in the pool, or, if necessary, lead a few songs or preach a sermon.

After breakfast, the daily schedule called for everyone to sit in the multipurpose room ostensibly for announcements, a devotion, and some light entertainment. What actually happened was that Austin and his friends fooled around with a trio of puppets—Cameron, Ron, and the Other Guy—on stage while the entire camp watched from metal folding chairs. The boy-men ad-libbed scripts based on their own inside jokes and a running gag where one of their puppets was perpetually "missing" and they traded accusations about which one of them "kidnapped" their absent felt friend. Most of the male campers thought these antics were cool, but the girls were bored, and why shouldn't they be? Every superhero who made an appearance was male. Everyone with a microphone: also male. And the puppets? Yep. Boys. The adult women reacted either in silence or whispered outrage. In short, it seemed that no woman in the camp had a scrap of agency, and I decided something had to be done. Families were paying for an actual camp experience for their children—male and female.

As one of the camp trustees, Scott had been milling around for a couple days. Arguably, he could have stepped in and steered the boys toward better behavior, but I don't think that was his style, or, perhaps, he had an idea of his own brewing—I'll never know. What actually happened was, the morning of the third day of camp, I looked Scott in the eyes and said, "Something is about to happen to those puppets."

Scott lifted an eyebrow and nodded. "Interesting." He drew out the word in the manner one does when invested in an impending plot. Scott and I knew each other well enough for this exchange to suffice as an entire conversation. He knew I was about to change the camp's dynamic, and I knew he was going to allow it to happen. I instinctively knew there was a chance things could go wrong and get ugly. I wanted to shake up the good-old-boys' network, but I also wanted a safety net. I wanted to know that I wasn't going to be sent home in shame like a camper caught in midnight hijinks. I wanted assurance that my escapades wouldn't become the topic of a meeting, the minutes published and posted for community viewing.

So I left breakfast early and tiptoed into the large multipurpose room. I slipped in a side door next to the stage area, and there they were in full repose on a low shelf: the puppets—all of them. I grabbed the most obnoxious one, a bespectacled character that I thought was Ron, balled him into a sweatshirt, and ran as fast as I could back to my cabin. I zipped Ron into my suitcase and shoved it under my bunk. I then went to the multipurpose room, took a seat, and waited.

Austin's eyes popped open as his gaze bounced from one of his cronies to another. "He's really gone." I read his lips as he mouthed the news to his pals, who all began whispering and shrugging. They seemed shaken. They limped through the morning meeting before dismissing everyone for activities.

Excitement circled camp as everyone began to realize that Austin and his friends really didn't know where their puppet was. Wanted signs were posted; rumors swirled.

Austin summoned me to the air-conditioned office. My son was sitting there with a popsicle.

"I think you know where my puppet is."

"Your puppet is missing? Which one?"

"Ron. He's gone, and I want to know where he is."

"Is he the one with the mustache?"

"No, that's Cameron."

"I can't remember which one is which."

Austin turned to my son. "Have you seen your mom with any of the puppets?"

Brandon licked his popsicle and shook his head.

"There's a whole freezer full of those if you see anything, Brandon." Austin sat down at the table, running a hand over his mop of unkempt hair.

I sat across from him, maintaining eye contact.

"I want my puppet."

"Tell me again which one is missing? The one with the mustache?"

"Why do you keep saying that?" Austin looked like he might cry.

I was unmoved. Austin was outside of this game, and I was going to leave him there for a while. The power dynamic in the camp was shifting, and I wanted Austin to experience uncertain terrain. "Listen, I hope you find your puppet. In the meantime, you can leave my son out of this," I said, shooing Brandon and his dripping popsicle from the office.

By dinner, word spread through the camp that a mock trial would take place that evening in the multipurpose room. Widely regarded as a suspect, I kept a low profile all afternoon. Scott maintained a poker face.

The mock courtroom crackled in excitement. Witnesses were called, speeches given. Everything was initially in good fun, but there was a definite moment when proceedings took a southerly turn. I remember two things about how the evening ended. Looking back, I can't construct a timeline that makes sense. I have an image of my suitcase being rolled down the middle aisle, alongside another scene where one of Austin's friends, a minister from a partner church, was grilling one of his students—someone I didn't know—on a "cross-examination." I saw my suitcase being opened and Ron held aloft. Then I heard the other minister ask the student a wildly inappropriate question involving the girl's father and something he may or may not have done to fall out of favor with their church. As the first tears trickled down her checks, Scott ended it. Court was adjourned.

Everyone spilled across the wide-open lawn. Scott was talking with the guy who made the girl cry. I was dealing with Austin and a couple of his friends who wanted to know why I found it necessary to kidnap Ron.

"I took your puppet because you have forgotten that there are girls here. The campers need to see female superheroes. They need to see women with microphones. And you need to realize that girls are here to play too. We won't be ignored."

The guys seemed shaken. One even apologized. Eventually, camp settled, the canteen opened, and snacks were consumed. Although camp didn't instantly transform, the angst lifted. Order was restored.

In the years that followed, I have twice run into girls who were at camp that week. "You're the one who took their puppet," they said. "We loved it." One of them called me an icon. I'm thrilled that there were girls at camp who got it. Years later, they remember the event as a takedown of what one of them called "the frat boys of church." But even though I loved speaking up, and I recognize that I wouldn't have gone through with it without what I then regarded as "top cover" from Scott, I question the notion that I ever had a true safety net. I have since grown to doubt that church, as a corporate function, can really be viewed as a safe space for anyone to land.

Around the same time, my husband was going through his own doubts about church life—about doctrines, policies, even standard interpretations of scripture that, in his mind, didn't line up. Although it would be logical to think that we bonded over our growing disillusionment, that would be far from the truth. Brad's questions made me feel angry and unsettled. I may have begun to notice and resent church "bro" culture, but straying from the foundations on which it was built was unthinkable. We were church people, damn it.

Among his many issues, Brad was developing a growing concern for what he referred to as "edge cases." What happens, he wondered, to people whose personalities are altered by brain injuries in ways that push them from or draw them to faith? What about mental illness? Depression? Schizophrenia? If faith could wax and wane with body chemistry, what did that mean?

"It's like you are looking for reasons not to believe!" My anger thinly masked a growing fear that we were falling away. I was aware that constantly butting against the lines put me on the brink myself. I was struggling to stay within the confines of acceptable thought because outside those lines was nothing but what, as an art teacher, I would have called "negative space." Lines, or "positive space," defined a picture. I was fine with adjusting the lines, extending some and completely erasing others. But entering that endless expanse of undefined space—that was the definition of being "lost."

I didn't know then that Brad's concern for "edge cases" marked the beginning of his ability to see a larger picture, an acceptance of the space around the lines as a necessary part of the image itself. I couldn't see his concern as the beginning of his own interest in personal narratives, of embracing a faith that played out in small scale—one individual at a time, fighting to find their place in the image, looking for someone to say, "I'm here. I won't let this go bad." Just add brownies.

15
Tyler

HAVING FAILED THE GAY COMMUNITY in church, in print, and over the air-waves, I seemed in no danger of becoming an effective ally. But the failures and the belief systems that led to those betrayals stayed with me. And the next time a boy explained to me that he was gay, I had the opportunity to do better.

Tyler met my daughter, Allison, when she enrolled at the Christian high school he attended. They were both in the drama class I was teaching at their school that semester, and they clicked instantly. They enjoyed books and shared opinions on classmates and teachers. He loved hanging out at our house. He fit in there; he got the jokes. He loved our cabinet of board games, and he took to our newest kitten. With no small amount of relief, the fourteen-year-old realized that all this meant that Allison was his girlfriend.

But Allison's idea of a relationship differed from Tyler's in one major way: she was constantly trying to hold his hand, to lay her head on his shoulder, to snuggle up to him—gestures Tyler never seemed to reciprocate. A snapshot from this time shows the two of them seated a few feet apart on our sunroom couch, their joined hands resting in the gulf between them. Allison is beaming with pride, leaning toward him as if to fill the gap; Tyler is smiling, but looks wooden, stiff, battling to hold his ground.

Then one day, it simply ended.

Allison was in tears when she climbed into the car after school. She didn't want to get up the next morning, didn't want to face the questions, the whispers as the news of their breakup filtered through the small school community. I sat at the foot of her bed, stroking her silky brown hair, an ache in my heart echoing the pain I saw in her limp form sprawled across her bed.

"He thinks he might be gay. Why would he want to be with a boy instead of me?" Tears welled in her brown eyes.

I knew, from chats I'd seen on the family computer, that Tyler was wrestling with this issue, that he was confused—frustrated that he couldn't will himself to feel different, to be different. But that was no help when my daughter was crushed, and frankly I was miffed by how much I would miss him too.

Although we still saw Tyler several times a week in drama class, a wall of tension went up overnight. But he was still my student; we were still in rehearsals for a play. There were lines to be run, scenes to be blocked, characters to develop. Accordingly, we functioned on set and ignored our real-life drama. Then the play ended, summer came and went, and most of the next school year passed before Tyler reinserted himself back into the structure of our home. He and Allison began talking again at school, and by the time summer vacation started, he was simply back like he never left, save for the absence of hand-holding and the fact that our kitten—at this point a full-grown cat—refused to forgive him. She's lived sixteen years now and has never forgotten the one year he was gone.

One afternoon, I was busy at the kitchen counter while Allison and Tyler sat next to each other at the farmhouse table behind me. They kept exchanging looks, catching each other's eyes. Allison mouthed something to Tyler that he waved off. I pretended not to notice.

"Mom," Allison finally said. "Tyler has something to tell you."

He stared at her wide-eyed, incredulous that she'd just thrown him into the spotlight.

"I'm gay." He blurted the words in a rush of pent-up energy.

I was surprised only by the sudden, jarring nature of the announcement. Of course I knew, but in a way the admission was news to Tyler himself. As his words registered, I smiled, relieved that nothing was actually wrong. "We can handle this."

Allison shot him a look. "I told you." She looked toward him and then back to me. "He doesn't want to tell his parents."

"But don't you think they know?" I slid into the chair directly across from Tyler. From my perspective, nothing here was breaking news.

"A couple years ago they found some messages on my computer," Tyler said. "I was trying to figure out what was happing with me, so I started going into some online chatrooms. I met an older guy who explained that I was probably gay. It all made sense."

I nodded. This was the story I, too, had seen the year before on our computer.

"My parents sent me to a Christian counselor who explained that I was confused, that I wasn't gay. They told me the guy online was a pervert. A dirty old man." Tyler paused to gather his thoughts, his long, brown bangs flopping in front of his eyes. "I was so relieved when I met Allison. I figured the counselor must have been right. I needed to give it time. I wasn't gay after all. But then the feelings started coming back."

I glanced at my daughter, gauging her reaction. This was the part of the story the three of us shared, the point where Tyler's adolescent quest for identity bumped into Allison's—but in that moment I saw only compassion and support in my daughter's expression.

"My parents think it was all just a scare, something in the past. No one has mentioned it in two years. I don't know how to tell them. They'll just send me back to that counselor. I don't want to go back!"

"We'll figure this out," I said. "How can I help?"

"I'm not ready to tell my parents yet, but can we just keep talking? Maybe do some research and come up with some ideas about how to help them understand?"

Despite a patchy track record of failing both a flesh-and-blood teen and a fictional camp counselor, I had somehow earned Tyler's trust and confidence. As an ally, I was far from perfect. I said some stupid things. I still held some problematic beliefs. But I was continuing to learn, even as we talked in the following weeks about Tyler's first kindergarten crush (on a boy who both kids knew then, as high schoolers), consulted scientific and spiritual sources about what was known and what wasn't about homosexuality, and spoke about how he might broach the topic again with his parents. In short, I was giving Tyler the kind of support I wished I'd given Steve years earlier in youth group.

Listening to Tyler that summer gave me a gift too—a bonus son. At some point during those weeks when he was asking questions; building courage; giving his thoughts light, air, and space; he became the "middle sibling"—between Allison and her younger brother, Brandon. Tyler became a fixture in our home, joining us for meals, events, and family outings. We spent hours that summer walking a beach near our house, a stretch of sand and surf left untouched by both the city and developers. We soaked in the sun, gathered trinkets that washed ashore, and talked. A lot. One scorching afternoon in early July, Tyler fell into step with me. "Will you call my mom?"

"Okay." I paused a moment as I anticipated what was coming. "What do you want me to tell her?"

"Can you just have her come with my dad over to your house? Just tell her that I have something important to talk about but not until they get there."

Tyler's mother, Amanda, and I knew each other but weren't close. The intensity of the circumstances seemed to circumvent the typical social niceties and protocol I'd typically worry about. I didn't consider if this was a good time to call, whether I'd vacuumed, or what I had on hand to offer for refreshment. I simply got her on the phone.

"Amanda, I'm with Tyler right now and he has something he wants to talk with you and Ray about. He's hoping you could meet us at the house in an hour. He's okay," I rushed to add.

"He can't... you can't... tell us what this is about?" Amanda fumbled over the jagged edge in her voice.

I turned to Tyler and raised my eyebrows. He shook his head.

"He really wants to talk with you both in person."

An hour later, six of us—Tyler; Allison; Amanda and her husband, Ray; Brad; and I—gathered stiffly in my living room. Brandon, it was later discovered, was listening through a vent in the upstairs hallway. Amanda and Ray, both Southern Baptist NASA engineers in whose presence I felt slightly intimidated even in the best of circumstances, entered the house in a pall of silence. Ray, whose beefy build and bearded face gave an initial stern impression his warm, brown eyes immediately belied, sank into Brad's recliner. Everyone else filed across the couch while I handed out glasses of water.

"Tyler, what's going on? Why did you call us here?" Amanda's voice was thin and shaky.

In measured, careful tones, Tyler told his parents what he had been explaining to us for the past few weeks: the feelings hadn't gone away.

Amanda sat quietly, tears streaming down her face.

"This again?" Ray sighed in exasperation. "We dealt with this a long time ago, Tyler." He paused for a moment. "We need to go back to the doctor."

"Dad, we've done that. I don't want to go back for any counseling."

"There might be a medical problem, something easy to fix—low testosterone, or something."

Tyler scoffed. "That's not it."

"What do you think is going to happen here? Do you expect me to invite your boyfriends over to dinner? You want me to buy them sweaters for Christmas?" Ray's voice boomed through the room. He'd ventured from fear to frustration and now, anger.

The conversation paused. I pictured Tyler with his arm around a boy pulling a woolen sweater from a festive box as Ray beamed. The thought cheered me but seemed incongruent with the moment.

"But didn't we raise you to know this was wrong?" Amanda's voice was paper thin, anguished.

Although I was solidly on team Tyler, I hurt for Amanda at that moment. I didn't have to wonder what she was thinking. As both a mother and a person well versed in mainstream Christian culture, I knew she was terrified. She was scouring her memories to figure out what she did wrong, wondering if there was still time to fix it. She feared for his soul. How would I feel if this were Brandon? I wondered if my pragmatism stemmed from having no real skin in the game. Although I was growing to love this kid, what was at stake here wasn't my family's future or worries over a son straying from the church.

The conversation reached a stalemate. In tears, Tyler went outside to the hose where he'd abandoned his shoes after the beach. Allison followed him out. Brad and I saw Ray and Amanda to the door.

"Here's what helped me understand," Brad said to Ray. "What if someone told me that the way I feel about women is wrong? If Tyler feels about men the way that I feel about women, how likely is that to change?"

Ray nodded and shook Brad's hand, but he didn't look convinced.

"My concerns for him right now are spiritual. The important thing is to nudge Tyler closer to faith instead of pushing him from it," Brad said.

In our private conversations, Brad and I returned to this idea often—our hope for Tyler to sense that faith was something still available to him, something that could be a source of strength. Ray and Amanda thanked us for spending time with Tyler and headed to the car, their son trailing behind them in tears.

I'd like to say that from that day on things got steadily better. I'd like to report that both Tyler and his family came to terms with the realities of his life and that that afternoon was a turning point. I'd love to say that Tyler never broke another girl's heart in an effort to be the son his parents wanted. I wish I could say that it wasn't Allison who gambled her emotions in what would be Tyler's last attempt at a "normal" life. It would be beautiful if I could write about how Tyler found comfort, wisdom, and support in a faith community.

What I can say is that the actual story of Tyler, his family, and mine is much messier and far less linear. It involved hard lessons, many tears, and large doses of forgiveness. The truth is that Tyler's ability to be at peace with both himself and those he loved wasn't found in hardline dogma or adherence to immutable doctrine. It came from humbler and less tangible sources: a cold afternoon stringing Christmas lights on my roof, a bouquet of rainbow balloons, and, yes, festively wrapped sweaters. In short, peace came via the usual route: love.

16

Identity

It was late August, and the window for me to find a job, any job, was narrowing by the day. It wasn't so much that I needed to work in a practical, keeping-food-on-the-table sense. Brad was making decent money as a government contractor, and my professional activities the prior decade had consisted of teaching art part time and writing for the newspaper. My first love was family life—camping and biking, vacations and car games, laughter, wet tents, and blown tires. Being present for these moments was the thing I wanted most out of life, but I knew it wouldn't last forever. I had to diversify. My first art position marked a golden period: I was teaching at my children's elementary school twice a week and chasing freelance leads for the paper the remaining days. I was a sort of educational Mary Poppins, floating in, usually at midday, with crayons, paints, and clay, and then fading out after a hasty cleanup to conduct interviews and meet deadlines. The money wasn't good, but I'd found my niches—my places to belong and thrive.

These roles were touchstones—tangibles I could claim as facets of my identity. I was an art teacher, which in the hierarchy of a tiny elementary school community equated to rock-star status. I'd arrive on campus to the students' cheers: a crush of little bodies with open arms as I pressed my way to my classroom, juggling supplies. I was also a writer, penning human-interest stories about big moments in ordinary lives, both the stories and the telling elevated by ink. It was a wave I could have coasted forever, but, like any crest, this one too tossed me ashore. The school and the newspaper simultaneously ran out of money, and suddenly I was neither an art teacher nor a reporter.

Unmoored and spiraling into depression, I turned myself in for a few therapy sessions. After dissolving into tears in the middle of a story involving some van Gogh finger puppets I saw in a gift shop but didn't purchase because there was "no-*sob*-reason-*wail*-to-*sniff*-anymore," the therapist suggested I look into taking a master's-level class.

"Start with one," she said. "And who knows? You might find something that will serve you very well for the next twenty-five years."

And so it was that I headed to nearby Christopher Newport University on a cold, dark January afternoon, expecting to return with cold extremities and, perhaps, an informational brochure about classes I probably couldn't afford. Instead, a chance encounter ended with an offer from a professor in need of a graduate assistant. I came home with a full-ride scholarship and a monthly stipend. It was both a miracle and a save. I had a new role to cling to: graduate student.

The master's program was designed to accredit K–12 teachers, but I was determined to leave with enough credits to qualify to teach at the university level. I still wanted the office, the campus, the students at my farmhouse table, ideas circulating and pasta spinning around forks. I wanted conferences, panels, and lectures. I wanted, perhaps unrealistically, a life I might have been planning for while I was cutting and pasting and camping and freelancing. It seemed I was the inverse of the cliché career woman suddenly pining for babies as she approached forty. I'd been a career parent; now I wanted the position. Perhaps this is our collective fate as humans: to always want one more thing.

Upon graduating, I asked the English department chair to keep me in mind if she ever needed anyone to teach freshman composition. I knew it was a long shot, but that long shot represented my entire reason for investing two-and-a-half years into the teaching program. I had to ask. Instead, I found my way back to teaching art: this time at a swanky, high-end academy.

If a tangible opposite exists to the instant-home feeling I have found in certain places, Swanky Academy piped it through their HVAC system. It wasn't that the student body was almost exclusively made up of the children of our community movers and shakers—the sons and daughters of high-volume real estate agents, car dealers, and defense attorneys. It wasn't the country club faculty meetings, or the Friday lunch-time wine and cheese bars in the hallway, complete with disposable china and gold plastic utensils.

My discomfort was rooted in something more basic than outward affectation. It was a pervading sense that there was a game afoot and I was, simply, without the rules—a theory that was quite literally confirmed when a pair of giggling colleagues burst into a lesson on lines and shapes waving a sheet of paper between them.

"Will you sign this?"

"Um, why?"

"To show that we were here."

I realized my blank confusion and annoyance were an affront to their frivolity, but I was dumbfounded.

"For points," one of the women offered, as though explaining multiplication to a right-brained third-grader.

"For the game," the other added.

I didn't know anything about the game, and I never would. I wasn't privy to the scoring system or what was at stake, but I had a strong sense that whatever was being tallied on my colleagues' scorecard was part of a larger tournament of expectations that I was never going to meet.

I signed on the line they indicated, realizing only much later that the signature I used summed up my entire problem at Swanky Academy.

I wonder, now, years later, if it was my instant not-at-all-at-home feeling that caused me to work at this school using another name. At the time I would have said that I always wished I had a different name, and this new environment gave me a chance to reinvent myself. Looking back, though, I can connect the dots pretty easily. I was never going to be known here. I would never be accepted. Something in me knew I'd have to be someone else inside those walls.

"Call me Kate," I said the day I was hired.

"Cate with a 'C'? Or is it your middle name?"

"No. Just call me Kate. With a K." Kate forgot names. Kate was reprimanded for not participating in faculty extracurriculars, such as "the game." Kate didn't even get a glowing classroom observation, something anathema to Cynthia. Kate was a terrible teacher for the simple reason that I wasn't Kate. I wasn't even trying to be—I was simply me, in an environment that would have never supported who I actually was: someone craving authenticity and community in a place where even spoons needed false veneers.

I don't think I realized just how badly I was performing as Kate until her contract wasn't renewed. And that's how I found myself, in the summer of 2011, again without a job, without a plan, coming unmoored.

Home was still my anchor, but my role felt increasingly tentative. The constants in our house were Brandon; his best friend, Conor, a tall, spindly tech genius still years away from admitting to anyone, let alone himself, that he was gay; Tyler; and my daughter, Allison. And I lived in the center of their collective orbit. And although Brad and I had long since wrapped up our time as youth leaders, our home still swelled with teen activity. The teen girls' Bible study I organized was still going. Over the years, my girls invited their little sisters and younger friends; later, some of my own kids' friends joined in, creating a teenage downline the magnitude of which would cause a multilevel marketing maven to burst with pride and residual income. Our rambling bungalow was a hangout house where everyone was welcome. But that year my girls were all seniors, and it had become clear that there were simply no more younger sisters or friends take their places. I came to realize that after thirteen years, there wouldn't be any fresh faces come fall when our longtime members left for college. Brandon, Conor, and all my girls were graduating. Allison and Tyler were already in college. Everything was ending, nothing was beginning, and I was manic.

Manic for me meant throwing energy in myriad directions and repeating until something, anything happened. I took to my art space and created a series of large mosaic seahorses. In terms of a potential career path, I am still not sure what I was going for as an end game, but I listened to a lot of techno-pop and spent the better part of ten days covered in grout. When the seahorses were completed, I loaned them to a pirate-themed restaurant where they spent the rest of the summer on display.

I asked my editor at the indie newspaper for more stories, secretly hoping she might consider early retirement and ask me to take the helm. I connected with a pastor on Craigslist about the possibility of creating an art gallery and coffeehouse. I also auditioned for a gig as a lifestyles reporter at a local TV station, through an annual competition called the Face of Fox. FOF was a multi-part contest with a year-long contract as the prize. Judging from segments I'd seen featuring the incumbent Face, the job involved a backstage pass to the entire Hampton Roads vicinity: Meeting animals at the zoo! Backstage at rock concerts! Behind the scenes at Busch Gardens! Every day would be an adventure and I would be a local celebrity. Heady stuff. Oh… and I also applied for a handful of regular public-school teaching jobs as backups, just in case.

And now I had an early afternoon interview for one of those backup jobs as an English teacher at a magnet school. The morning of the interview, Brandon, Conor, and my visiting nephew, Paul, hopped in my van to go for a stack of eyepatches (you might know them as pancakes) at the Pirate's Booty, the marina eatery where my large-scale seahorse mosaics were on display, before I dropped them off at carpool for day camp. We settled around a table at the pier.

I kept checking my phone. I knew it was too early to look for an update on my Face of Fox tryout, but I'd been wound up since early the prior evening when I got an email from the TV station marked "urgent." I'd made the first round of cuts, and "at least one producer" wanted headshots and additional bio info immediately. I flew into an excited frenzy, not least because I lacked current headshots.

I had texted my friend Cat, who worked at the TV station as a regular reporter and had encouraged me to enter the contest in the first place. She'd rushed over with a camera and a MacBook and, after a blur of outfits and lighting adjustments, we had headshots that almost made me feel like I had this one. But the thing about headshots is they're just images: slice-of-the-moment glimpses of fleeting truths, incapable of telling the full story or showing the bigger picture, which, in my case, was that the head in perfect focus in those shots was about to come unglued.

We submitted the requested materials in time for what I imagined as an *American Idol*-type scene with photos strewn across a boardroom table and producers arguing the merits of their top picks. The names of the contestants moving ahead were going to be read live on air—right about the time I had to drop the boys off at the carpool. Thus the constant refresh as I waited for Cat's text.

Teaching high school English could be rewarding, but for me, at that moment, it felt like giving up, settling on poring over students' words instead of writing my own. I also feared I would never get an MFA—the degree I actually wanted back when I settled for a free master's in teaching. I'd never teach university. Perhaps these fears were overblown. But that's not how they felt as I sat at the table on the pier, sipping coffee, dipping eyepatch bites into syrup, and glancing at my phone.

I finally felt my phone buzz on the highway after I'd dropped off the boys. "Didn't make cut."

I remained stoic. I'd been surprised to have made it as far as I did. But learning I was not destined to be the Face underscored the gravity of my afternoon interview. The dread I'd been trying to outpace all summer was closing in around me. I had been waking up more and more often with a familiar lead weight in the pit of my stomach. I kept throwing more and more energy into action—any action holding the promise of relief from the fear creeping into my psyche, the voices telling me that I had to have a role, an identity, even one that wasn't quite right.

Arriving home, I stepped into the shower. I'd just rinsed the shampoo from my hair and was reaching for the conditioner when I first realized something was wrong. My mind scrambled to make sense of the hundreds of brown lines swirling around the floor of the tub like a monochromatic Jackson Pollock. I instinctively reached for my head, and I gasped in horror as I realized my hands were covered in clumps of long, dirty-blonde hair, hair that was still falling from my head in terrifying amounts. I sank to the floor of the tub, gathering it all into a pile as panic sucked the air from my lungs and seized my throat, my heart, my limbs. I knew I was coming undone; I just hadn't expected to have to see it happen.

All summer I had worried who I would be without kids in the house, without a job, and now, possibly without hair? Nothing seemed secure.

I went through the motions of getting ready for the interview and driving to the school. I remember sitting in a small office with a kind, if not slightly desperate, middle-aged man. I remember the questions being easy; school was looming and he had a position to fill. I got it: life was looming and I had an internal crater to stuff. It might have been an easy match. I couldn't tell you; my mind was too busy choreographing every movement: *Don't gesture. Don't nod. Don't shift in your seat. Don't let the rest of your hair come unglued right here in the principal's office.*

I know he offered me the job and that I must have accepted it, but the next scene that is clear in my memory is me behind the wheel of my van, sobbing. I'd like to say that my visceral reaction was a wakeup call, that I realized I really didn't want to be a high school English teacher, that it occurred to me that I might not be in the best shape to make big decisions, but that is not what happened. Instead, I talked to HR, filled out some paperwork, and a few days later received a thin, white envelope—my contract. We were heading out the door as the mail arrived, on our way to an end-of-summer vacation in Florida. I tossed the envelope on the kitchen counter. It could wait, I figured, until I got home.

Several days into the Florida trip, we trooped back into the hotel room from the pool in stages of wetness from dripping to damp. I picked up my phone and saw I had a message. A moment later I sank to the bed in disbelief.

"Brad?" My voice shook. "I have a message from one of my old professors at Christopher Newport. They have an emergency opening. She wants me to teach freshman composition."

Three years later, and she had remembered. And just like that, the other life I'd described to the elderly parishioner around the Baptist church boardroom table found me after all. I was, suddenly, a professor.

I was too excited and, frankly, starstruck, to register any downside of taking on a job as an adjunct. I'd been back from Florida less than twelve hours before I found myself at a boardroom table with many of the professors to whom I had so recently submitted papers, delivered reports, admired as role models. I knew I would be making less than half of what I would have as a high school teacher, but this felt way cooler. I knew, intellectually, that I likely hit the ceiling on what I could accomplish professionally the moment I signed my one-semester contract (with a verbal promise of continued employment). I guessed that eventually I'd want to move on, but for the moment, I was feeling pretty giddy about the whole thing.

It would be a couple of semesters before an incident from my graduate school days emerged from the shadows of my mind. I had been making copies for a professor in the same room I now, as an adjunct, made copies for my own students, when a spry, balding man of long tenure, a professor we'll call Dr. James, entered the workroom. He introduced himself before asking about me. I told him who I was working for and that I was in the teacher preparation program. "Oh, so you want to teach high school?" he said.

"No," I answered. "I want to teach college."

Dr. James frowned and shook his head. "Sounds like you are in the wrong program."

I knew my program wasn't an ideal match for my endgame but it had quite literally chosen me. I also knew that, if not perfect, my degree would still get me the credentials to teach at the university level; I knew both the limitations and the potential of my decision.

"I'll have the credentials I need to get a foot in the door somewhere." I tried to keep my voice light, my tone nonchalant. I didn't want to admit, to Dr. James or myself, that he'd hit an exposed nerve.

Dr. James frowned. "No one aspires to be an adjunct."

I GET A SENSE ABOUT certain places. Every so often I walk into a new place, and I know, instinctively, there's a place for me here. This is home. I felt it the first time I walked into the round church where I became a youth leader. I felt it at the private elementary school where I sent my children and became an art teacher. And I sensed it on my son's Bible college campus when I brought him for a high school senior tour and, somewhere between the morning song service and the ice cream parlor visit, I thought, *I could teach here.* I shook the idea off. It was ridiculous. The commute would be daunting and I was in my first semester of teaching at Christopher Newport. How would this little school fit in to that? And then, eighteen months later, an adjunct left the Bible college and there was an emergency vacancy. My son, who was then a sophomore, had his psych prof tell the dean that his mom could teach, because that's the way things roll at the quirky little university with rustic buildings, a close-knit student body, and kumbaya campfires that made the tiny campus feel like endless summer camp. And just like that, I was a professor at two schools.

Besides, I needed the tuition money now, not just for my son but also for me. I had just enrolled in an MFA program because as much as I loved professor life, I now understood Dr. James's assessment about adjunct teaching and why my opportunities were coming to me as "emergency openings." Adjunct life is tough. No dreamed-for office, insulting pay, and, worst of all, tenured professors kept taking my classes if they failed to fill their own. I wanted to see if I could go further with an MFA.

I traded my van in for a brand-new, jalapeño-green Chevy Spark I dubbed Pepito. Teaching at two schools and doing my own work as an MFA candidate at Old Dominion University in Norfolk meant that my life now played out at three universities, through two bridge tunnels, and across one state line. It also meant Pepito was my office. The interior was like a messy dorm room on wheels—a haphazard collection of clothes, shoes, papers, and the remains of the previous day's takeout. I'd grab a veggie bagel sandwich at Einstein's, the CNU coffee shop, at noon, and a latte at a well-worn hole-in-the-wall where the beans were fresh roasted and the staff knew my order—in North Carolina—by evening. Or I'd write at home all morning and brave the notorious Hampton Roads Bridge-Tunnel traffic in the afternoon in time for my four o'clock workshop at Old Dominion University, grabbing a bagel-hummus sandwich from the library café as I ran to class.

Life felt snappy and full of potential.

17

The Inlet

STU OPENED A SMALL DRINK cooler and withdrew a frosty can of beer. "Only sixty calories, but really good! Here, try it." He lobbed a can my way. I'd recently adopted Stu's weight-loss plan and had fallen into the habit of keeping a mental calorie tally of everything I put in my mouth. Sixty calories seemed a bargain with the afternoon sun beating down on our flotilla on the James River. We'd just navigated a few low-grade rapids and were now bobbing along a gentle stretch of water. As I popped the tab on the can, Elaine announced, "Stu has a theory about Dani."

A new teaching gig wasn't the only thing my son brought into my life. Brandon had a chance encounter with a campus visitor at one of his school's late-night bonfires that led him to a job as a teenage music minister—at a church that was somehow a few football fields away from our front door. It had been there all along, but somehow I'd failed to recognize the small warehouse at the corner across from the Walgreens as a church. But when Brad and I went to check it out to make sure our son hadn't been drafted into a cult, we discovered the Inlet, a vibrant congregation. They were a diverse assortment of NASA scientists, doctors, drug users, and folks experiencing homelessness, with a quirky, sixtysomething pastor in sandals at the helm. The congregation quickly became our community, our people. It had been years since we integrated so fully into a group: weekly dinner at Elaine and Stu's, Saturday softball games, texts, and coffee and crafts. In Elaine I'd found the peer—fortyish and active with grown kids—that I'd been craving to befriend. With a personality as untamed as her mane of wavy auburn hair, she teetered the line between bossy and fun. But since she also had a propensity for adventure, I embraced the fun.

The advent of softball season brought us in closer contact with our newish friends, Dani and Joanna. Dani, a heavyset woman with close-cropped hair who did nothing to accentuate any feminine features, lived with Joanna, a blonde with bright blue eyes, a big smile, and a stocky build, in what appeared to be a full domestic partnership. In addition to a house, the pair shared a car, vacations, and even a goddaughter who would stay with them in the summer and attend the youth group they co-led.

Our community fathomed Dani and Joanna with the same understanding that we, as a society, have long held concerning *Sesame Street*'s Ernie and Bert. I always assumed that they were lesbians, and my budding friendship with Joanna had, over the past year, included conversations with enough cues and clues that it was no surprise when she finally revealed that she was Dani's partner. Throughout the spring, however, Dani had been sporting shorter hair, larger shirts, and baggy cargo pants—adopting such a masculine stance that Elaine upended the entire lesbian theory that summer afternoon on the river by suggesting that perhaps Dani was trying to tell us something else altogether.

"Well, you know those surgeries Dani's had ..." her voice trailed.

"I know she had one," I said. "Last winter."

"Well, she's been looking more and more masculine lately. What if it's related to the surgery?"

"What? I don't think so," I said. "She had a hysterectomy."

Elaine raised her eyebrows meaningfully. "What if there's more to it?"

"Like a sex change? Really?"

"I don't know," Elaine said. "I just don't think she's really ... female."

❧～❧

DANI AND JOANNA LIVED IN an old, rambling bungalow a couple of blocks from the beach, a place Joanna had called home for her entire life. Although

Momma Miller, her octogenarian mother, still owned and lived in the home, Dani and Joanna ran the household. They were the decision makers and bill payers, even though Momma Miller's mark was stamped on the home's décor. Baskets and bric-a-brac adorned every inch of interior real estate. A large, stuffed snowman stood sentry, year-round, in a corner just inside the front door. His subordinates, a set of cheerful magnets, conducted their collective watch on the dishwasher door.

But it was Momma Miller herself who supplied the bulk of the home's atmosphere. She was well known for the "Momma-isms" that Joanna often posted on social media as the "Momma quote of the day"—outrageous comments that ran the gamut from comically mixed-up words to the politically incorrect musings of a mind set in an earlier era.

I don't remember when I first started going to the house, but I would realize long after I was there for the last time that it corresponded with my response to a seemingly unrelated cultural event. Months before I'd spoken more than a few words to Dani, before I even knew the word *intersex*, and long before I could even conceive of a circumstance where my son's university would pursue me for a tenure position, Facebook added a feature that simultaneously confounded and offended many of the platform's users. The tumult was ignited by the social media behemoth's decision to update the gender options available for users to include in their profiles. The comments I saw on the upgrade ranged from amusement to vitriol, but the theme of all the posts was universal: on the question of gender, there were just two answers: male or female.

My first thoughts weren't of principle, but of a person: the ambiguously named Capri, a server at an Italian restaurant we frequented. Tall and board-thin with close-cropped hair and a glittery belt buckle, Capri served up bread and pasta with humor and verve.

"I like him!" I said to Brad, the first time we sat in Capri's section.

My husband narrowed his eyes in confusion. "Who?"

"Our server. He's so friendly and funny."

"Our server is a woman," he said.

"Uh, no. Absolutely a man."

In the heat of the Facebook flap, I realized the likelihood that some identifier on the list of new gender options probably described Capri, a friendly, funny person who worked minutes from my home. I also realized that the commenters all probably new Capris, too, but regarded them as aberrations, freaks, people who made poor life choices. But this dialogue seemed off to me. It simply didn't mesh with my understanding of Jesus's teachings about love. It seemed suddenly important to say something. But how, and to whom? And, more troubling, at what cost?

The lessons I internalized about church communities taught me to skirt controversy. *Communities cannot disagree. People leave if your experiences differ from theirs. I'm in danger when I disagree.* To disagree meant to risk being discounted, excluded, removed. My ever-present fear of potential ousting fostered a need to be liked, to be admired, to be perceived positively all the time, by everyone. These lessons loomed large over my interactions—and my social media. Although I prefer to view myself as a bold, outspoken woman, the truth is that when it comes to aligning with something likely to result in a social shunning, it's a safe bet that I'll just keep quiet. But some combination of indignation over the moral outcry over gender identity—the literal existence of a segment of the population—and feeling secure at the Inlet made me want to try out my voice. So I took a deep breath and pounded out a long post about why I thought sensitivity toward gender identity should matter to Christians—and I waited for the proverbial sky to fall.

Instead, Elaine commented about how her influence had been *so good* for me—she'd made me bolder, braver! And I got a thumbs-up from Joanna. It would occur to me much later that my indirect, unknowing affirmation of Dani had encouraged Joanna to seek my friendship. Suddenly, Joanna began engaging with my social media posts. In time, messages would pop up with pictures of crafts or recipes—"Hey! Want to try this sometime?" I usually did. Often, we would.

Vegetables would appear, unbidden, at my door, sometimes followed by a text to the effect of: "Got too much squash in my farm share delivery this week—I need help eating them!" More often, I'd get a string of pictures on vegetable delivery day, not unlike a series of botanical mug shots: "Can you identify these?" Being a vegetarian, I was usually able to positively ID the produce. Occasionally unfamiliar vegetables presented a challenge; I'd look them up and we'd make plans to try new recipes.

⸏⸏⸏

JOANNA HIRED BRANDON TO BE Momma Miller's chauffeur for the summer, a Morgan Freeman–type role he was well suited for, thanks to his love for history and those who lived it. In addition to driving her to the biweekly morning shifts she still worked at the city's main library, Brandon would shuttle Momma Miller—walker and all—on errands around town. "It's just like hanging out with grandma all day. We go shopping and watch TV and she talks all about the old days." Brandon's reports gave us an additional dose of Momma Miller-isms, and from Joanna we received secondhand rave reviews from Momma Miller about her new "grandson."

Meanwhile I was becoming increasingly curious about Joanna's relationship with Dani, and I wondered when—or if—she would ever directly address it, or if I was simply expected to gather up the clues she dropped into our conversations. Then again, there was always the chance I read too much into offhand remarks, like the day I posted an account of a large spider I'd battled in my sunroom and she responded with a story about an equally terrifying bug dropping from the ceiling onto her face one night, and Dani emerging from slumber to kill it. My mental picture of the scene suggested the pair had been in the bed together. It shouldn't and didn't matter to our friendship if Joanna was a lesbian or not—but I saw her as a witty, generous woman with long-term friendship potential, and I wanted insight into the basic facts of her life.

Another day, Joanna was telling Brandon and me a story about Momma Miller that included an aside about the older woman's belief in traditional gender roles. "She still thinks dinner should be on the table when a man comes home from work. She's even like that with Dani." Joanna laughed.

"Not that Dani's a man," she rushed to add. The remark was odd, but, in my mind, it was a communication. *She's trying to tell me that Dani's the butch lesbian,* I thought.

That idea seemed confirmed when she texted me a cockeyed picture of her and Dani taken on a weekend getaway. "Could you straighten this for me?" she asked, drawing on my reputation as a sometimes-photographer. In the photo, Joanna was uncharacteristically in a dress, beaming beside Dani, who had donned a full suit, complete with a tie. I laughed in delight. In that still frame, they looked like a comfortable, out, lesbian couple. It was beautiful, I thought, to see them happy, and to think that maybe society was changing enough that they felt they could enjoy their relationship openly. In this assumption, my photography training failed me. The hours I spent editing unwanted litter from street scenes and pesky cowlicks from portraits, the time I invested in making skies bluer and water more vibrant, had somehow not taught me that a snapshot is, simply, an illusion.

But it was within the context of this illusion—of Dani and Joanna as a longtime lesbian couple on the cusp of social acceptance—that my family became invested in their lives. One evening that spring, Joanna invited our family to dinner.

Dani entered the kitchen through the back door and padded barefoot across the sloped floorboards wearing floppy cargo shorts and an oversized T-shirt, balancing a plate of sizzling steaks and portobello mushrooms. The table was abuzz with topics that doubtless included Momma Miller's running commentary on Brandon's love life.

"Don't be marrying any of those Haitians!" she'd admonish Brandon on a near-daily basis in the months leading up to our annual trip.

Joanna laughed. "Now, Momma, give Brandon a break. You didn't like that girl he brought over a few weeks ago."

Momma snorted. "Too much makeup."

Food began circling the table. I was wary of the mushrooms—I'd always found them slick and slimy—but Joanna told me that Dani, worried about accommodating my vegetarian diet, had been researching recipes all afternoon. I slid my steak knife through a bite-sized bit of mushroom, coating the blade in a thick, dark sauce. I poked my fork through the mashed potatoes before gathering the bit of mushroom, as a taste-bud buffer should the mushroom prove unpleasantly earthy, but the starchy mask was completely unnecessary. Dani was an apparent grill master.

The empty plates had barely left the tabletop before the focus shifted toward a stack of board games on the hutch just behind Dani's seat in the cramped dining room. Dani began highlighting the merits of each before we settled on a word game with high comedic potential. Before Dani had distributed the various cards and tokens across the table, a short young woman with shoulder-length, curly brown hair came into the dining room, set a plate of cookies on the table, and slid into an empty chair. I recognized her as Krista, a college student from the Inlet who only attended when she was home for breaks.

No one seemed surprised by her appearance, but my chronic low-grade social anxiety seldom permits me to view the introduction of a new person as a good thing. I hadn't thought anyone else was joining us, and I wondered why she was suddenly at the table. Then I remembered the amount of people who come in and out of my house, occasionally without even knocking, and I felt instantly comfortable thinking of Dani and Joanna's house as the same type of safe-haven gathering place as my own. Plus, she brought cookies.

Krista folded seamlessly into whatever game we were about to play, and the evening went on as if she'd been there from the start. She didn't say much, and I wouldn't have occasion to think of her again for several months. But I left hours later with a neatly packaged grilled mushroom and the feeling that our community had expanded—again.

18

Panera

BRAD AND I WERE SITTING in one of our favorite pizza places one mid-October evening when I wasn't in North Carolina, Norfolk, or holed away with a giant mug of coffee and a bowl of popcorn tapping out a paper.

I'd just started my second year in the MFA program, and I couldn't really say things were going all that well. I'd entered the program on a portfolio of journalistic human-interest stories and a few essays I saw as witty. I wanted to do my thesis as a collection of humorous essays, with an eye toward becoming a Nora Ephron or a Sloane Crosley—funny women who lived their adventures and took readers along for the ride. But those intentions had been squashed the prior semester when a visiting professor of some renown steamrolled over my workshop submissions in a cloud of scorn and derision. I elicited some laughter from him, but it wasn't the mirth I was going for.

"I wish you'd turn your lens on some of the darker elements of your life," he said, snorting in disgust over an essay I'd written involving a yard sale, a bike named Biff, and some elementary school kids in the market for overpriced cotton candy and B-roll rides at a traveling carnival. He called me into his office for a secondary thrashing where he treated me to a personal reading from his recently released memoir, selecting a passage detailing a family member's suicide and the subsequent tumble his mom took from the toilet upon hearing the news. When finished, he slammed the book shut as an indictment. *There. That's how it's done.*

Things were so bad I was considering singlehandedly erecting a structure on some abandoned wooded property we owned and attempting to live off the land until I either had a story or succumbed to the elements. I wish I were kidding.

Brad and I were in some sort of discussion about the general state of my academic woes when my phone buzzed. *Elaine.*

"Can you swing by Panera real quick? Please?"

I thought about ignoring the text but decided to just shut it down instead. It was date night. I couldn't bring myself to deal with her. Things between Elaine and me had radically changed since that early summer day on the James River. Although I always knew Elaine's personality toggled between bossy and fun, I'd spent two years embracing the fun and ignoring her more domineering behaviors. But the life-coaching program she'd completed late that summer shifted the balance toward the domineering, ultimately changing her relationship with the Inlet and with me. By fall, she was barely attending and had all but coached herself right out of our lives.

"I'm actually nowhere near Panera—already ordered Italian."

"Okay. Well, Dani is here with me and wants to share something."

"Is she okay?"

"Actually, that's what he wanted to talk to you about. He's great." Elaine had my full attention now.

Dani was now Danny. This was important—for Brad and me, a drop-everything-and-run sort of affair, not unlike the obstetrician's midnight call to the delivery room or a first responder summoned to the epicenter of catastrophe. Someone at that moment needed exactly what we had to offer. We boxed up our pizza and headed to Panera.

Sometime after we absorbed Tyler into our family, Brad and I began to quietly fall into a role of support for queer people. It was more like an underground railroad situation than in any official capacity. We liked to send word out through our networks that we had a place at our table and a bed in our home for anyone in need of a safe space. And now that someone needed us, we were on it.

Danny offered a nervous smile as Brad and I slid into the booth across from him and Elaine, but he quickly turned his attention to a napkin he was twisting between his fingers.

"So, Danny's ready to start sharing some news with people. I told him that before we started this," Elaine waved a hand vaguely between her and Danny, indicating their private sessions, "you and I had a strong hunch about what was going on. Danny's really nervous about how to explain things to people, so we've been working on a script, and I promised him you guys were safe people to practice on."

Brad and I both smiled at Danny, encouraging him to go on.

Danny smiled nervously and cleared his throat. "Elaine said I should start sharing this gradually in small groups, with the safest people first so I can build some confidence." His voice quivered, and he paused and stared into the twisted napkin as though he'd find the script printed somewhere in the folds.

"So, you've probably heard the term *hermaphrodite* before. It's actually called *intersex*, and it refers to people who have both male and female sex organs. That would describe me." Danny pressed his lips together in a tight smile and nodded, looking me straight in the eyes. He took another deep breath. "All my life I've identified with my male side, but I've had to present myself in the way that people wanted to see: as female. But I've recently decided that I can't do that anymore, and I'm going to live the rest of my life as me, as a man." Danny's voice became more confident as he spoke. I was internally cheering him on.

I don't remember what Brad and I said, but I know we affirmed Danny in a way I wish I had been equipped to affirm Steve and even Tyler. I recall Danny relaxing and smiling. I remember Elaine slipping out.

"Goodbye!" she waved. "Have fun! And don't forget to send me those referrals!"

Don't forget those referrals? It was like she had just brokered a real estate deal. Seeing her for the first time in months, I had briefly lamented the gulf that had grown between us. As she toodle-ooed out the door, I remembered why it happened. I turned to face Danny—who clearly represented the future of friendship for me.

When we finally stood to leave, I knew two things: Brad and I had a new friend, and we were going with him on a journey into spaces the church never equipped us to navigate.

19
The First Night of My New Life

SEVERAL DAYS LATER, BRAD AND I were driving back from a long weekend in the mountains when my phone began to ping with a flurry of texts from Danny. "I want to tell my parents tonight about me. Can I come to your house first? I want to review and pray."

Despite the seriousness of the situation, I couldn't help but smile at the thought of Danny "reviewing" his scripted material. It had been a week since I sat across from him at Panera as he furrowed his brow and twisted his napkin like a school kid summoning lines for a class pageant. It would be a while before he was comfortable going off-script and having a natural conversation about a topic he'd kept locked away for thirty-some years. I knew he'd feel more comfortable with a fresh rehearsal under his belt before driving across town to see his parents.

A second wave of texts came in from Elaine, who, along with Stu and Joanna, would be going with Danny to talk with his parents that evening. We agreed that everyone would meet up at our house first to give Danny a good pep talk before he faced his family.

Elaine and Stu were the first to arrive, stepping around the post-camping-trip maze of drying tents and tarps we'd draped over our garden fence and around the yard in front of our oft-expanded 1930s-era house. They walked in without knocking, a leftover habit from the heyday of our friendship. The tension that came through the door with them that evening, however, had nothing to do with the four of us. It stemmed from a sense that from here, there was no turning back.

"It's not just his family," Elaine said. "He's really worried about church. He's afraid that people aren't going to want him to continue working with the youth."

This didn't sound right to me. "But doesn't everyone already think that Danny and Joanna are a lesbian couple? I mean, there's no way I am alone in this. If people are okay with lesbians leading the youth group, how are things worse if Danny and Joanna turn out to be just an ordinary hetero couple? What's the problem?'

"Because they never identified themselves as lesbians," Elaine said. "People might suspect they are, but no one has ever been sure. People are willing to let it sit. Besides, they really aren't even a couple now."

But I knew Danny and Joanna were a couple. Joanna had told me how they had been married, secretly, eleven years before. How they had a big party and called it her birthday celebration but it was really their wedding; how they'd exchanged vows privately, just the two of them. She told me they'd fought recently, but they were working things out.

Maybe Elaine doesn't know that I know about that, I reasoned.

Joanna was next through the door. Her complexion was sallow and her voice as thin and filmy as a piece of tracing paper. "He drove separately." Joanna's jaw barely moved as she spoke. "When it's over, he's going to call her."

Elaine adopted the matter-of-fact tone of a parent repeating a snacks-before-dinner policy. "We have talked about this. You need to let it play out."

Tears spilled from Joanna's eyes. "I should be the one." She spoke through her teeth, seething.

"You'll be there at the meeting," Elaine said, in a way that was either soothing or patronizing; I couldn't decide. Who was Danny calling? Why was this a problem? I suddenly felt like a character dropped into a story in medias res. My role, beyond playing host in the scenario, was suddenly a mystery.

Everyone froze when the screen door creaked. Even through the mesh, Danny's face was sallow and corpselike. This wasn't summertime-barbeque-and-board-game Danny, or zany youth leader Danny covered in mud or marshmallow. This wasn't even sick-to-the-stomach-nervous Danny I'd sat across the booth from at Panera a week earlier. The person who came through the door wore the glazed expression of someone whose life was about to permanently change, perhaps not for the better.

My confusion was quickly forgotten once Danny sank into my sofa. Brad, Joanna, Elaine, and Stu wordlessly filed across the sectional. The silence was painful. I don't remember who broke it, but I'm willing to bet it was me, selfishly wanting to wiggle out from beneath the weight that had settled in the room.

"You'll get to have some questions answered," I said, grasping for something positive. "What is the thing you want most to know?" I asked.

Danny's death mask softened into something resembling a thoughtful expression. He looked at me as though I'd said something wise. I would grow to love that about Danny—the way he always takes what I say seriously, like my ideas really matter to him.

"I just want to know if they ever knew. On any level. Ever."

The question was, indeed, one of the mysteries of Danny's life. It made sense that, regardless of the answer, he'd want that question resolved. But we also knew he was terrified that the conversation he was about to have would result in an outcome he'd lived his entire life trying to avoid: being a disappointment to his family.

I knew Danny had every reason to believe the next hour would end in disaster. He'd been living as a woman for over three decades out of fear. He never told his family because he knew rejection was almost assured. He had no reason to expect acceptance now, but something foundational had changed in Danny. He had come to the place where his survival depended on risking everything he thought he couldn't live without.

We understood that our role now was to reinforce the rightness of his decision and bolster his confidence, so we pumped Danny up the best we could and said a few prayers before he, Elaine, Stu, and Joanna left for Danny's parents' house on the other side of town. I stayed and put cookies in the oven, because there wasn't time for brownies and I don't know how to navigate a crisis without fresh baked goods. I chilled some hard cider, settled into the couch with my laptop, and waited for him to return with his story.

~e~a~

"IT'S AN UNBELIEVABLE STORY," DANNY said, hours later, taking a swig of his cider.

"You couldn't even write a believable story about how crazy his life has been," Joanna added.

The four of us sat for a moment, absorbing the details of Danny's evening with his parents.

"My wife could," Brad said. "My wife could write the story."

I scrunched my face in disapproval. Of course, I *wanted* to write Danny's story. How could I not? I was on a fast track to living in a hastily constructed shack and writing *Walden* meets *Into the Wild* for my MFA thesis. But it seemed presumptuous and awful to co-opt a story in which I played a bit role. Before I could actually deliver the daggers my eyes had formed, I realized Danny and Joanna were both smiling and enthusiastically saying, "Yes!"

"No one is talking about this," Joanna said.

"Would you do it?" Danny asked.

I felt a dozen things at once: excitement, inadequacy, and also a sense that this decision would be a sort of "coming out" of my own. If I wrote about intersexuality and gender transitions, I could never again be opaque about my views on sexuality if I found it inconvenient. I'd no longer have the ability to just say nothing—everything would be out there, in print, for the record.

"Yes!" Excitement flooded through me. This was better than the collection of humorous essays, and way better than slapping up a makeshift structure in the woods and seeing if I could survive on the land. This was a project that could mean something: for Danny, for others like Danny—and for me too. This was definitely it!

I didn't know then how quickly my resolve would be tested. I had no way of knowing that the next week tenure would somehow be on the table or that I had just altered the course of my life—and, like Danny, in ways that might send my life wildly off-course. I'd forgotten about Krista, and I had no idea why Elaine had claimed hours earlier that Danny and Joanna weren't even a couple. Although I had a vague notion that we'd all just made some decisions from which there could be no turning back, I was mercifully unaware that we were as far away from a satisfying ending to Danny's "unbelievable story" as a group of people could possibly be.

❧

LATER THAT WEEK IN NORTH carolina, I refreshed the weather app on my phone for the dozenth time. My students were tapping out their final responses to a writing exercise in the computer lab, and it was almost time to head home. The commute had lost its early-fall luster—the golden sun playing along the rolling green horizon, the crisp air whipping in through Pepito's windows. My return trip was now a path sliced through darkness, and tonight the specter of a storm loomed in the forecast. I knew I needed to leave immediately after class if I had any chance to get ahead of it, but Mitchell, the academic dean, had approached me on my way up the stairs earlier in the afternoon and asked if we could talk after class.

He'd emailed me the day before about an emergency need to hire a full-time English professor, asking if I knew anyone who'd be interested. A routine accreditation review at the university had ended in a mandate for the hiring of a full-time English professor. For a second, I half-jokingly thought about pitching myself as a contender—but I'd barely begun my MFA, and grinding a circuit from North Carolina to Norfolk then to my home on the Virginia Peninsula, day in and day out, wasn't physically possible. The fatigue and dread over the potentially treacherous miles between my classroom and my bed were evidence of that. Besides, I thought, *I've barely begun my MFA. I haven't started my thesis.* I couldn't imagine I was that stellar of a candidate, and I didn't want to embarrass myself.

Still, Mitchell wanted to chat. I decided to dismiss everyone a few minutes early so I'd be ready to talk when Mitchell arrived. The students filed out with their usual end-of-class comments, questions, and stories, and then Mitchell, a fortysomething with square glasses and thinning blond hair, popped in and sat down in a spot where a student had been only moments ago.

"So, we're looking for a speedy appointment to this position," he said. "I'm hoping you could make plans to be here for a full-day interview. I'm thinking within the next ten days, if you can make the time."

I sat across from Mitchell, resisting the overwhelming urge to say, "Wait—you're actually interested in *me* for this?" Because he clearly was. He was quite obviously sitting in front of me asking me—dare I say persuading me?— to come to an interview that sounded an awful lot like a formality.

I rallied my professionalism and asked a few questions. Did he know I wasn't close to finishing my MFA? Did he know I still needed to attend evening classes?

Mitchell must have interpreted my questions as hesitation, because he began talking salary and benefits. "We want you to finish your MFA," he said. "In fact, we need you to. I'm thinking we'll have you on campus twice a week and then teaching another course online. It's a rare tenure-track appointment, and I hope you'll consider it."

My head was spinning. Could this be real?

❧

"You coming, mom? Makenson's about to start." My phone lit up with a text from Brandon as I finished a simple crackers-and-cheese dinner in the small apartment right off the student lounge. Less than two weeks had passed since that conversation with Mitchell, and now, here I was, the night before my full-campus interview—an interview that was seeming increasingly to be a formality—staying in an apartment off the student lounge and wondering if this was the beginning of a whole new life.

"On my way," I texted back. Makenson, the Port-au-Prince native who a handful of us had befriended the previous summer during the stick-maybe-tree mission trip, was spending a week on campus as a prospective student. He was about to host a Haiti Q and A in the student lounge. I instinctively swapped whatever I'd been wearing for the green Team Haiti shirt I'd stuffed into my suitcase and walked out the apartment door into the lounge. Makenson, an early-twentysomething with a huge smile and boisterous laugh, snuck up behind me and gave me a hug. Out of the corner of my eye, I saw a cluster of green shirts—Brandon and the rest of the team. No one had talked about changing; we all just had. One of the students slid to the edge of his chair and I joined him on the wide seat. I felt like I was home. I felt like I belonged.

That night I fell asleep to the sounds of student laughter on the other side of the apartment wall. I realized this could be the first of many nights like this, staying over on campus for events, campfires, late-night chats. This could be the first night of my new life.

20

The Boardroom

I SLID INTO THE HIGH-BACKED vinyl chair across from Mitchell's desk, grateful to be wearing black. The dark fabric masked the stickiness—part nervous perspiration, part fortitude—that was seeping from my pores. Arguably my entire life had been moving toward this moment. A tenure-track position had fallen, mid-semester, in my lap, and I was about to throw it all away.

I could almost see it as I crossed the lawn on the way to Mitchell's offices: the job, the office, and, remembering an offhand comment Brad made about his ability to telework—the possibility of moving into one of the enormous old houses flecking the surrounding neighborhood. By the end of the day, that all could be mine: that unlikely other life—the storied old home, the splinted farm table, the students, the pasta—it had all somehow found me after all.

The rightness of that feeling made me wonder, again, why I needed to mention my thesis project at all. Why invite trouble? But I knew at my core that if this was ever going to work, I needed to be accepted completely—views and project included.

Now, in Mitchell's office, I was going to launch my first trial balloon and see what came back.

"Before we go up to the boardroom," Mitchell said, steepling his hands as he leaned back in his chair, "are there any other questions you have about the position?" I'm sure Mitchell was expecting something light, perhaps the day's agenda for my full-campus interview or details about my responsibilities. But

I'd already asked those questions. I already knew that the schedule and the courses I'd be teaching and developing were a perfect fit. I already loved my students and couldn't wait to have my own office where I'd host afternoon happy hours with coffee and chocolate and tutoring, and where I'd establish a revolving, open-door atmosphere of conversation and encouragement. I knew all that. What I didn't know was how much of myself I would get to retain in exchange.

I took a deep breath. "Thanks for sending along the faculty handbook last week. I was particularly interested in the section on intellectual freedom and publishing." I paused in an effort to avoid regrettable phrasing—or fainting, neither of which was out of the question. I took solace in the fact that the handbook promised that faculty could expect to enjoy "full freedom to write and to speak as a citizen and a person" so long as their views did not "compromise the integrity of the university."

It's sad to think that a condition of birth could threaten the moral fiber of an academic institution. Worse, that my employment could be in the balance over a condition that wasn't even my own. But I speak fluent church, and the party line on issues of sexuality inferred that a lot more was at stake than the reputation of a mere university. The intellectual freedom clause of the handbook had gone on to say that the range of acceptable thought allowed for "differences in the interpretation and application of scripture on matters that do not undermine the foundations of the Christian faith." So my question was if, in the view of the university, my academic and personal interest in Danny's transition represented foundational cracks that could cause the whole system to crumble.

"The section interested me in light of a manuscript I am working on about intersex and transgender people." I paused, considering the possibility that enough had already been said, before adding, "in the church."

Mitchell went blank, as though disabled by an invisible switch. Seconds ticked by before he rallied. "Why," he asked, "would you ever be interested in writing about *that*?"

Because transgender teens are disproportionally homeless? Because nearly half of transgender adults attempt suicide at some point in their lives? Because hate crimes against trans persons are becoming a staple in the news headlines? Because the church is the one institution to which these statistics should matter most? Although any one of those reasons should have been sufficient, I went for the personal narrative.

"I have a friend who appeared female at birth but inside, always knew he was male. In puberty, he even developed male sex organs. But he lived his entire life until now as a woman, because he was afraid the church wouldn't accept him for who he was."

"So you're just telling this person's story?" Mitchell asked, a hint of hopefulness in his voice. I imagined Mitchell's brain already working to reframe the situation into something palatable. Although the handbook clearly stated that permanent, tenure-track faculty must be "members in good standing" at a church of a particular denomination—which the round church was, but not the Inlet—he'd found a loophole that satisfied the higher-ups. Although my MFA was still two years in my future, he'd carefully reviewed state standards to prove I was qualified to teach and lead in the areas where the university needed me most. And he'd drafted a schedule that had me at the university three days each week and teaching online from home the other two. In case that wasn't enough, he'd reminded me that Brandon's tuition would be waived, padding the already decent salary by an additional 20 percent. Mitchell wanted me for this job. Maybe he'd find a way around having a professor with a progressive view of social issues.

Still, I realized I was Mitchell's top pick by default. I knew it was a function of being at the right place at the right time. Even as an adjunct with a regular master's degree, I was the most, perhaps only, qualified person currently connected to the campus. In his need to maintain the college's accreditation, how far was Mitchell willing to stretch?

"I'm not yet sure of the full extent of my project," I answered honestly.

"But would there be any, er, evaluation?" Mitchell asked.

"Evaluation?"

"Would you be offering opinion or commentary?"

"Well, again, I don't yet know the scope of the project, but I would like to be in a position to freely explore the issue without stipulation."

Mitchell nodded and glanced at his watch. "I think it's best that we just continue this discussion upstairs," he said. "We'll have to see what Peters thinks."

I'd never actually met President Peters, although, from scant forays into his social media postings and stories from Brandon, I couldn't picture him enthusiastically endorsing anything that could be construed as progressive. But I wasn't about to prejudge. I had already confessed that I considered myself "socially liberal" and supported pro-gay legislation during a prior conversation, and I was still in the game. I reminded myself that people are more complex than we often realize—that no one can be summed up by a title, or role, or even an ideology. Our understanding of life adapts to allow for integration of new experiences and information, and I wanted to believe that was true for the faculty at this tiny school as well.

I followed Mitchell up a staircase and through a maze of hallways, taking in features of the architecture despite my nerves. The campus was the exact kind of quirky I am predictably drawn to: places like the Inlet, or the gym I deliberately drove to with the cracked floors and half-dozen obese members in the seedy part of town. These things work for me; they remind me that life plays out in all kinds of places, and they give me access to stories and people that challenge my mind and encourage my soul. And although I was quite happy at Christopher Newport with its manicured Great Lawn and columned buildings, I could easily see myself making a professional home at this little school.

The Bible college campus was just a few small brick buildings and a row of old, rambling houses—the charming kind with winding staircases and skeletons of strong hardwood—and a large brick building. Faculty and various administrative offices were nestled inside the houses. The large brick building was the center of campus academia. It was a maze of classrooms, study areas, and offices connected by staircases and hallways that emitted an olfactory experience—a mix of dust, wood, and character—that is typically the domain of antique shops and the better estate sales. The décor consisted of seventies-era portraits of beneficiaries, pull-down maps, and the occasional sepia-toned, standard-issue depiction of Christ—the one that looks suspiciously like a free eight-by-ten from an Olan Mills sitting.

With a student body hovering around two hundred and a penchant for unconventional norms, such as renting out dorm rooms to nonstudents to pad a perpetually precarious budget (and a recruitment program that drafted at least one of my remedial students off a local beach), the school wasn't your typical four-year university. And that's part of what I enjoyed about the place.

Mitchell kept walking ever deeper into the upper floor of the building until he stopped at a room that boasted the largest table I have ever seen. It seemed as long as my dead-end street, and about as wide. It wasn't a stretch for me to picture the entire freshman class sitting comfortably around its polished surface. "This isn't at all intimidating," I said.

Mitchell laughed. "The others will be joining us in a moment," he said. "I'm expecting Peters, Jim, Catherine, and Kent."

Peters I knew only by reputation, but I had never even heard of Jim. Catherine was a stout, elderly woman who was at the helm of payroll and IT. My only personal interaction with her had been about a year earlier when I went to her office with a question about a faulty piece of campus software and she yelled at me because she thought I was a student and, as such, had no business with the software or in her office.

Kent was a psychology professor who had been to my home for dinner about a year prior, when my son and his daughter briefly dated. He'd also helped me sneak backstage when a popular band visited campus months earlier and a power-hungry coach-turned-bouncer kept shooing me away. I hoped he'd be as helpful in the current context.

Peters was a robust septuagenarian with wire-rimmed glasses and a quirky tie. He entered the room with a clipboard and a crisp, businesslike air.

Jim introduced himself as the vice president and provost. He looked to be in his late sixties, with warm, brown eyes and a quick smile that almost made me forget that I was moments away from a discussion about my friend's genitalia.

The purpose of the interview was for these key personnel to get to know me better as a person before joining the staff at large for an academic interview in another hour. The questions were easy enough in the beginning. Kent wanted to know if I thought an increased role on campus would create any challenges with my son. "Maybe you have some tips," he said, referencing the fact that his daughter, now one of my composition students, had begun her first semester as a student on campus.

"Nah. As you know, Kent, I started working here in the first place because my son suggested you all hire me. We're really close and know how to communicate."

"You've been with us a couple of semesters now," Peters observed. "What do you like best about things here?"

"The diversity of the students, and a chance to really make a difference. The students I have in my basic English class aren't your typical college students; my class might be their only chance to go forward and get a degree." The diversity of the school is a source of pride; the university had recently been recognized as a leader in providing scholarships to disadvantaged students. About a third of the students were minorities, around a fourth were adult learners, and at least a dozen hailed from far-flung parts of the earth. Most of these international students were missionaries, or the offspring thereof, and many focused on gaining education to take back to their countries of origin. The students in my remedial class—like Kevin, who'd gone from being a local beach bum on Saturday evening to a degree-seeking undergraduate by Wednesday—had academic records that would preclude their acceptance at other universities. The flip side, though, to the school's "everyone gets a chance" philosophy was that the average incoming freshman lasted just one semester. When their next question was about my perception of institutional weaknesses, I discussed this point and some ideas I had to help. With each question, I could feel my confidence escalate.

Catherine peered over my résumé. "You've done a whole lot of things," she said. "I'm just wondering if you'd be happy settling down here."

Realizing the possibility that my résumé might cast me as a beatnik dabbler—*I teach art! I'm a youth leader! I write things! But never in the summer so I can go abroad!*—I rallied to shift the question into a springboard. I launched into the story about my long-held aspirations of becoming a beloved professor.

Peters jumped in. "Since you live a distance away, have you put any thought into how you might recreate that sort of situation within these perimeters?"

"Yeah, actually, I have," I said, telling him about my happy hour concept.

He nodded. "And you know we have the apartment over in the residence hall. Some of our commuting instructors like to use that every now and then, when we have campus events. Would that be something you'd like to do?"

I told him I'd stayed in the apartment for an event the night before and was hoping it would be an option that could continue to be available.

Mitchell cleared his throat. "Cynthia and I were talking earlier about our intellectual freedom policy. She wanted to clarify it in light of a manuscript she's working on," he said. "Why don't you tell the group what you shared with me down in my office?"

I swallowed hard. "Well, I am working on a project about intersex and transgender people. In the church."

The room was still. Faces froze. The polished table was the only thing in the room still beaming.

"Why this topic?" Peters boomed, laughing.

I paused for a moment and decided to channel Danny that night three weeks ago at Panera. I pictured the nervous smile he gave Brad and me as we slid into the booth across from him and Elaine, before he turned his attention to a napkin he was twisting between his fingers, wanting to practice his speech in a supportive environment.

Even though I wasn't at all sure that Peters was a friendly audience for me to practice on, I took a deep breath. "Maybe you've heard the term *hermaphrodite*," I said. "It's actually outdated and misleading, but when people use it, they typically mean *intersex*: someone who has both male and female organs. That describes my friend Danny. He was born looking completely female but always knew he was really a boy. He later developed male sex organs but was afraid to tell anyone because he didn't want to be rejected by the church, so he went on presenting himself the way people wanted: as female. But it's become too much for him physically and psychologically to continue living as someone he's not, so he's made the choice to live the rest of his life outwardly being who he has always been inside."

"*Whoo hoo hoo*," Peters chortled, bringing a fist down to the table and then his head right beside it. "Well!" he sputtered through his laughter. "I always say to my staff—when something happens, just tell me. I can handle anything, but you have to tell me. I sure didn't see this one coming, though."

I wasn't sure if this outburst was good or bad. It was hard to tell if he was, indeed, prepared to handle this revelation, or if he'd just stumbled on the one thing he really couldn't handle and was thoroughly flummoxed.

"Well, how often does something like this actually happen?" Peters asked, gathering his composure.

"About one in two thousand people are like my friend Danny. But studies show that approximately one in one hundred people are born with bodies that differ in some way from standard male and female binaries," I said, drawing on information I'd gathered from the website of the Intersex Society of North America. "It can be helpful to view it as a continuum," I said. "The truth is, you all know someone who is like this, but they are afraid to tell you."

"Is this true, Kent?" Peters asked.

Kent smiled at me as he nodded. "Yes, everything I'm hearing is right on," he said.

Jim had been hanging on my every word. "I want to read this book!" he said, his eyes flashing in excitement.

I glanced at Catherine, who had yet to say a word. She appeared to be stifling a smile. I pictured her mentally weaving together a good yarn to share over dinner. I had the distinct impression that nothing this interesting had happened in this room in quite a while.

"Is he getting any surgery done?" Jim asked.

"I think he wants his outside to match his insides," I said. "I believe he's planning a mastectomy." Later, Danny would explain the preferred term "top surgery," a procedure done with a focus not just on removing the breasts but creating "normal"-looking male chest contouring and nipple placement.

Peters waved a palm idly at the ceiling. "It sounds like that L…G… B…T…Q nonsense." He recited the letters slowly, as though picking them out of a particularly thick alphabet soup. "Where are you going for this MFA anyway?"

"Old Dominion."

"I'll bet they lo-o-o-v-e that!" Peters snorted. "Secular, liberal education. Do you support homosexuality?"

"Intersex actually doesn't have anything to do with being gay," I said. "And *transgender* refers to a person's psychological identity, whereas *intersex* refers to biological characteristics. Where those lines may converge isn't really known," I added.

"Well," Peters said, "it may not be gay, but they're certainly kissing cousins!" he blurted, then burst into gales of red-faced laughter when he realized what he said. The room broke down. Even Catherine began to laugh.

I wasn't sure what, exactly, was so funny. Personally, I found Peter's reaction to be absurd enough to warrant laughter, but it wasn't clear what amused him. Was it nervous tension?

Peters sobered. "But you understand what I am asking here," he said, looking directly at me. "Is homosexuality wrong?"

Here it was. The bullet I thought I'd dodged. The week prior, I'd been summoned to the office of a senior faculty member for what was referenced as the "full" doctrinal interview (to distinguish it from the lighter version I'd had when I was brought on as an adjunct). The office walls were seemingly held up by books—including a tome that must have had a full foot on the spine of *War and Peace*. The tenant of the office, a Bible scholar with large plastic glasses and a tweed overcoat that made him look like he'd been lifted off the dust jacket of a 1970s Bible commentary, asked me to join his colleague, a robust archaeologist known for his off-topic lectures and affinity for making mud bricks. Between the pair, they could cite the linguistic etymology of all scripture as well as the exact stratum of soil where the documented events took place. The rest of the faculty deferred to these men on all spiritual matters.

The linguist had sat at his paper-laden desk and gestured for me to take a seat on the sofa next to the archaeologist. I feared I was about to be grilled about homosexuality, a topic that had been conspicuously absent at my interview the year prior. The topic had loomed, unaddressed, in the recesses of my mind since the beginning of my employment. I knew enough about the ideologies of the school to understand that homosexuality wasn't a concept they championed; however, I took the silence on the matter as hope that a "don't ask, don't tell" culture could exist—a culture that just might make room for someone who didn't claim to have the answers; an environment that might allow me to quietly construct my now-familiar role as a bridge for the LGBTQIA+ students who I knew, from statistics and personal knowledge, existed on campus. These were my hopes. But the truth was that since the moment I was first asked to pursue the tenure-track job, I had expected my prospects to be over after this interview with the two professors. But when it ended after an odd line of questioning about the finer points of baptism and a few stray questions about the structure of my church, I allowed myself for the first time to believe that I might actually have a shot at becoming a tenure-track professor.

And yet, there I was, at an interview that had been billed as an elaborate meet-and-greet, forced to answer the question evangelical Christianity has somehow shaped into the ultimate litmus test.

I deflected to buy time. "It's wrong for me," I said.

"Don't play that game with me," Peters boomed. "Don't make me ask you the right question, in exactly the right words. That's the thing my sons always did that made me the maddest." His face flushed and his nostrils flared.

In an instant, I'd gone from being a professional woman on the cusp of landing a promotion to an insubordinate child in need of correction.

"You know," Mitchell intervened, "Cynthia probably hasn't had the opportunity yet to see the new Marriage and Family Statement."

Peters took a breath and smiled. "Ah, okay. Will you shoot that on over to her, Mitchell?" He tapped a pen on his clipboard, then looked me straight in the eye. "Why should I hire you?"

It was the easiest question they'd asked all day. "Because I don't know how long you're going to have to look before you find someone who cares more about the students than I do."

Peters's eyes betrayed his surprise at my bold statement, but then he smiled and nodded. "My first impression is that you'd be dynamite here. I may have some follow-up questions for you later. And Mitchell—get that document over to her right away."

Everyone filed out of the boardroom to reconvene in another building. Kent pulled me aside in the hallway. "If your friend would ever be willing to come to talk with my human sexuality class, I'd love to have him," he said. I wanted to view the offer as a statement of acceptance, but I knew Peters was far from satisfied.

The prospect of the statement loomed over the otherwise encouraging second round of meetings. I knew everything—the smiles, handshakes, and attractive financial package presented to me at the business office—would all vaporize as soon as I opened my email.

I stood on the sidewalk with Mitchell before I headed to my car to go home that evening. He expressed enthusiasm about the day's events. "I'm heading back to my office now, and I'm going to send that Marriage and Family Statement over to you. You're not going to have any problems with it," he said. "It'll be in your email when you get home."

The drive through rural North Carolina with the windows down just before sunset had become familiar to me over the past couple years. With a fresh cup of coffee, satellite radio, and golden sunshine sinking into farmland, it wasn't difficult to imagine myself doing it three days a week, ten months a year.

I parked in front of my house, grabbed my laptop, and ran to the living room, fingers flying across the keyboard as I entered various passcodes to access my campus email. I took a deep breath and opened the one from Mitchell with "Marriage and Family Statement" in the subject header.

The statement consisted of a thorough catalog of variant human conditions, to include not only all homosexuality but also "attempt(s) to change one's biological sex, or otherwise acting upon any disagreement with one's biological sex," followed by a hard-and-fast ruling that the entire list of ills was "sinful and offensive to God" and "repugnant to the principles of the University."

It took about a second of scanning the document for the truth to sink in. I was never going to be a tenure-track professor. Not now, not at this school, and likely, not ever. I stared blankly at the screen, willing the letters to rearrange themselves into words that were more gentle, loving, inclusive.

"What does it say?" my husband asked.

"That this is over," I answered.

Until now, the question had been whether or not I was willing to slide in under the radar, aware that the school probably didn't agree with my stance, but not really knowing the extent of their position and, thus, never having to actually lie. I'd been wrestling with both the morality and practicality of the situation. Was it wrong to withhold my opinions on a divisive issue? Wouldn't it be better to just be there for the students? Did I want Peters—a reported Facebook enthusiast—creeping on my social media posts? And, far more uncomfortable, how much of my decision was motivated by the financial reward the job would bring?

Confronted by the words on the screen in front of me, the issue became, literally, black and white. There's right. There's wrong. There are men. There are women. There's no gray. There's no confusion.

Until this moment, I'd been sitting at a commitment equinox: already one of Danny's frontline first responders for major developments, but in a role that required no personal cost beyond my time. I listened to Danny and cheered him on as he began the process of becoming more himself each day.

I helped him practice conversations that would change the course of his life, waving from the sidelines as he embarked on the journey of a lifetime—his lifetime. Balanced at the midpoint between spectator and participant, I had, now, the luxury of watching, albeit with concern, how things turned out for the principal players.

But now it was *my* future on the line. As humans in polite society, we know when it's socially acceptable to avoid certain topics. Politics, finances, a secret penchant for blaring Nickelback alone in the car—we all pick and choose what to reveal in various settings. I could retreat into vague statements of pseudoconsent and have a shot at becoming a well-loved professor like I'd always dreamed. Or, I could be brave, like Tyler, the youth group teens, and Danny before me, and take a step out into territory from which there would be no return.

Intersection

21

Coming Out

Danny

IT WASN'T DIFFICULT TO READ my parents' expressions as they watched the four of us, Joanna and I, Elaine and Stu—strangers, to them—approach the door. Their faces molded into the same expressions I remembered from childhood, the faces that communicated trouble, a fall from their good graces.

I introduced Elaine and Stu, and we all walked stiffly into the living room. My parents still lived in the house that had come with beaded doorways and puke-yellow walls, the home where the second half of my teenage world played out. I was stricken with the idea that this moment here, now, tonight might become my final memory here. "Elaine is a life coach who's been helping me with a few things," I said, trying to establish Elaine's role as a facilitator as we all settled into seats. When no one responded, I panicked and blurted the line Elaine gave me as an icebreaker. "The good news is I'm not gay!"

I was supposed to deliver it like a punchline, but it bombed. Mom went from frosty to utterly glacial. Silence descended on the room. I pivoted back on script and dove into my prepared material: intersex, always identified as male, going forward as myself. And when I finished, my parents sat in utter silence, motionless.

"I think I understand," Dad finally said. "This kind of makes sense to me. You were always muscular, liked guy things. I guess I have always thought of you as both."

Mom remained frozen in her spot on the sofa.

"I think he needs to hear that you're okay, that the news won't destroy your relationship," Elaine said, looking at Mom.

"Of course! You're my child!" Mom said, turning to me and ignoring Elaine. "Nothing is going to change that." Then she took a long, deep breath. "How do you know?"

"That's part of what I wanted to ask you," I said. "Did you know and not tell me?"

"No! I didn't know!"

"I changed your diapers," Dad said. "I didn't know."

Mom switched gears. "I was an LPN," she reminded me. "Tell me in graphic detail."

Not knowing what else to say, I just repeated my script. "You guys never noticed?" I asked.

"So, you think you are a man," Mom said. It was a statement, not a question. "Or you feel like one. How long have you had these feelings?"

"Mom, I have a penis!" I shouted. "Don't you remember that time when you asked about my sheets? Remember that embarrassing conversation?" The first time I had a wet dream and Mom confronted me with the evidence on laundry day was a moment etched in my mind forever, even if Mom never recalled it. I'd stammered through some sort of noncommittal explanation and then made sure my mom and my sheets never came in contact again.

"I think maybe I remember that," Mom said. "But you played with Barbies!"

"You gave me the Barbies! I wanted G.I. Joes. Do you remember the Christmas you guys gave me The Sunshine Family, and I had them all in crew cuts that night?" It had been an epic Christmas scandal: the mother missing an eye and the baby vanished. I'd transformed that set of dolls into something else, something closer to the infantry set I wanted. "You were so mad! Do you remember this, Mom? I made them part of the army!"

"Okay, okay, I think..." Mom's voice trailed off.

"It's going to take some time to process," I said. "But this is who I am. This is how I am going to live."

Mom sputtered and then suddenly remembered Joanna, sitting silent and stone faced. "Wait. Are you and Joanna—"

"No, we're just friends," I lunged at the question, allowing no opportunity for Joanna to enter the conversation. "She's here for moral support."

"I am so disappointed that you never thought you could bring this to us," my mother said. "We've never given you any reason to think..."

All our talks about Marty's identity and transition instantly sprang to mind. "But what about those conversations about Marty? You were so disgusted when I tried to explain it to you."

"You'll always be my child!" Mom was crying. "I prayed and prayed to have a daughter as my youngest, and God gave me you, my little redheaded baby girl: the answer to my prayers."

Dad reached over and gently put a hand on Mom's knee. "Sherry, I think we don't tell that story anymore."

I knew at that moment things were going to be okay. I was going to go forward in life as my parents' son.

22

Going off the Map

Cynthia

THE DAY AFTER THE MARRIAGE and Family Statement hit my inbox, I hunched over my laptop in a hallway chair outside the Christopher Newport classroom where I'd just finished teaching. I'd made a decision, and I needed to act on it while I still had the nerve. Adjunct life had made me adept at creating pop-up office spaces in stairwells, on benches, or on patches of chemically enhanced grass, so it seemed fitting to make my nomadic work life permanent on the berm of two-way, between-class hallway traffic.

Mitchell, I am so sorry to say that I will not be able to support the Marriage and Family Statement as it is written. So much of the time in these cases the only honest answer I have is "I don't know," and I have learned to be at peace with that answer. I am okay with not being in the position of judge, and focusing instead on what I know to be my job, and that is to love. My stance is to leave judgment to God and focus instead on the mandate I know to be clear: to love. I know this means that I will miss the opportunity to work with all of you, and that is heartbreaking.

I still don't know why I said, "as it is written." Almost as if it was an editing problem: *We were so close—just a semantic gaffe that I can't quite see around—can we revise? Perhaps a gentler verb here, a question mark there?* I probably soft-pedaled my response because I hated the thought of not leaving

166

some sort of opening for resolution, some hope that this clearly impossible situation could yet be salvaged and, somehow, I could just go back to looking forward to an office, a nice salary, and no tuition bills. I wrestled with varying versions of "good enough" answers, or ways to give them an evasive turn of phrase that would allow me to secretly harbor my beliefs without technically lying. Part of me wanted to do that—pretty badly, actually.

In the seconds before I hit send on the email that would end my tenure-track aspirations, I recalled a conversation I'd had with my father a couple days before my interview. His conservative phase was decades in the past, and we now enjoyed conversations about God and politics through a shared progressive lens.

I had sprawled out on my king-size bed and its typical tumble of pillows, blankets, husky, and cats and hit my father's number on my phone.

"Did these people come right out and ask what you were writing about or for your opinions on any of this?" he asked, after I'd brought him up to speed on my writing project, my upcoming interview, and my concerns about what would happen when they learned about my work, either up front or down the road.

"Not yet," I admitted. "But I know it's coming."

"You aren't obligated to volunteer anything, you know," he said, a familiar timbre of righteous, screw-the-man indignation in his voice.

Part of me was eager to explore this line of thought. I wanted someone to convince me that my fears were unfounded, that keeping some information close to the vest was not only human but also expected. I wanted to hear that it didn't really matter if I told them or not, that I could keep my work and private lives separate and still be a good person. My ears were itching to hear it—all of it. But no matter how hard I tried, I pictured the whole thing ending in a quasi-Amish shunning.

"I don't know, Dad," I said. "I don't want to have this thing hanging over my head all the time. They either need to accept me, my views, and my project or not, I think."

After a pause, he said, "If you do this, you can't become my friend Walt."

"What do you mean?" I asked, laughing.

"Walt fell in love last year with a woman named Kim. He decided to propose even though there were a hundred reasons why it wasn't going to work with Kim. She didn't want his golf clubs in the garage. She didn't like his friends, his clothes—the list went on. We'd sit at breakfast every week and he'd complain bitterly. Then Kim gave an ultimatum." My father paused for effect. Delivering the news across the airways for a living meant knowing how to pace a story for optimal effect. He also has a Christlike tendency to speak in parables, and I wondered where this one was going.

"What happened?" I asked, falling under the spell.

"Kim said no golf clubs. No old friends. Pare down his stuff. If he was going to be in her life, it was going to be by her rules."

"That's not fair."

"No, no it wasn't. Walt knew this, and he let her go."

"Good for Walt!"

"You'd think good for Walt," my dad retorted. "Until you have to listen to him. Every week, it's, 'How could I have let her go? She was the love of my life! I'm broken.' But you and I both know that life with Kim would have been a disaster." My father paused again. "This school is your Kim," he said, his speech building momentum like a preacher closing in on the altar call. "It's not something that's going to work. If you decide to tell them, don't look back. It's not the one that got away."

Not the one that got away, I repeated to myself days later as I took a deep breath and one last look at my email. My palms dampened and my pulse quickened, but I hit send and clapped the lid on my computer like it was the back cover of a rough read and headed down the hall toward the parking lot.

Mitchell must have picked up the its-just-a-semantic-difficulty vibe of my email, because the response I found when I logged back into my email later wasn't the "sorry to see you go" I was expecting. Instead, Mitchell emailed to ask the address of the Inlet, which he wanted to visit on Sunday "as part of the hiring process." Just as I concluded that Mitchell must have sent his email before reading mine, I read his closing line: "We'll talk more about your feelings on the Marriage and Family Statement in person."

I wasn't sure whether to be hopeful or offended. On one hand, was it possible that I had pulled this off? That I had laid my metaphoric cards across that beaming boardroom table and gotten this job on my own terms? Had I done that? On the other hand, it seemed more likely that there was a miscommunication, probably a result of my "as it is written" misstep, or worse, a feeling on their part that I was malleable or ill informed—that I could be talked out of my conviction.

I SURVEYED THE SUNDAY MORNING scene as I walked into the open room of café tables and string lights—the Inlet's version of a sanctuary. Brandon, who at nineteen had already been the Inlet's music minister for two years, was onstage warming up with members of the worship band. He stood in the center of the stage, clad, as always, in skinny jeans and a well-loved concert T-shirt, strumming his acoustic Taylor guitar. He was flanked on one side by a brooding male bassist, and the other by Chet, a thirtysomething, undermedicated bipolar vocalist known to leave the stage, sometimes mid-song, in the throes of rage or a sudden allergy. Danny kept time in his usual spot behind the drum cage.

People were filing in from the adjoining café area, balancing Styrofoam coffee cups and plates of donuts and greeting friends as they cut paths to their seats. Joanna waved and approached my table.

"Is he here?" she whispered.

"Not yet."

"Are you nervous?" she asked.

"Why should I be?" I asked, laughing, reminding her of some of the highlights from the boardroom scene I had described to her at our friend Andi's birthday party earlier that weekend. "Sounds like that L...G... B...T...Q nonsense," I said, waving a hand dismissively through the air while Joanna laughed.

"I have come with snacks," a voice boomed. It was Rob, a regular at the coffeehouse where my daughter, Allison, worked as a pastry chef. At her invitation, the husky, bearded history teacher began attending the Inlet a few weeks prior. "I don't know everything that's going on here. I just know someone is coming, we are nervous, and these are probably called for," Rob said in clipped, theatrical tones that served as his baseline timbre.

"Hey, it's the Customer!" said Pastor Dave, shaking Rob's hand. Dave dubbed Rob "the Customer," after Allison reminded him several times that Rob was not her boyfriend. Dave turned to me. "I hear we're under investigation this morning." His tone and inflection carried an energized, folky amusement that many Inlet members lovingly imitate.

"Yes, it seems we are," I shook my head, glad someone from my family had brought him up to speed since I last briefed him on the situation midweek.

"Well, I will try to be on my best behavior. I don't want to be the cause of anything bad that happens," he said, scrunching an eye and tilting his hand back and forth like an out-of-control seesaw.

I laughed. "Oh, I am doing a good enough job ruining things on my own. Nothing you could do will make it any worse."

Pastor Dave, whose jokes get him in trouble with his wife at least once a Sunday, may have worried that my employment prospects would be over by virtue of his sermon alone, but Brandon was more optimistic. The classes he'd taken with Mitchell had already involved discussions of different styles of "doing church," and Brandon said Mitchell had always seemed interested in learning more about our laid-back, church-is-for-everyone approach.

Seeing Mitchell out of the corner of my eye, I waved him over to our table as I opened Rob's coffee-shop bag.

"Yes!" I exclaimed as I saw Allison's signature oatmeal crème cookies— my absolute favorite. "Rob, you are amazing!"

We greeted Mitchell and forced a cookie on him as Brandon called the service to order. I was pretty sure that sitting at a café table eating fresh cookies while listening to a preacher in sandals delivering a sermon from a stool wasn't a typical Sunday morning for him, but he seemed unperturbed.

The service was uneventful by Inlet standards. Chet made it through the service happy and healthy, Pastor Dave avoided verbal gaffes, and Mitchell seemed pleased. He made some offhand remarks about the service to Brad and waved a hand at Brandon, still playing as people filed out of the room. "We need to wrap this thing up pretty quickly," Mitchell said. "Peters is pretty worried."

"He should be!" I exclaimed. I rejected his statement. Metaphorically balled it up and threw it back at him. I mean, I did, didn't I? Did he think I just didn't understand what I was saying?

"Well, here's what I'd like to do," Mitchell said. "I'd like to hold a conference call tomorrow afternoon with Dr. Raoul. He's our most conservative faculty member, and Peters tends to look to him on points of doctrine. If we can get Dr. Raoul on board, I think we can still make this happen." Dr. Raoul was the archaeologist I'd met with a couple weeks prior. He'd always been friendly to me, and my son enjoyed him as a professor, but both times I interviewed with him I noticed his tendency to fixate on minor points, hanging onto them with a tenacity that would have been impressive as a feat of endurance but became downright exhausting in an interview setting. I didn't see the situation going well.

"I have to tell you, Mitchell, that I don't see a way around this. I don't see a way forward here, but if you do, I guess I'll play this out. I'll follow your lead tomorrow," I said.

"Great! I still have a good feeling about this," he said, grabbing his coat off the back of his chair and heading to his car.

The good vibes were Mitchell's alone. The mention of Dr. Raoul all but squelched any flicker of hope Mitchell's optimism may have sparked. Since Mitchell initially approached me about the position, I had anguished about it more than I thought normal for something I wanted—or thought I wanted?— for so long. I struggled to figure out why. Did the permanence of tenure scare me? I'd heard it described as "golden handcuffs." Did I fear being locked into a position that wouldn't be a professional waystation, a stepping stone to something more, or better, or different, but likely my final landing place? Maybe. Or was it something just beyond conscious reach, like a passing flicker caught in the corner of the eye? That thing you hope was just a play of light or shadow? That thing I may or may not have seen a few weeks earlier when I sat by Dr. Raoul in the linguist's office?

We had been sitting on a nondescript brown couch positioned on the right-hand side of the linguist's desk—Dr. Raoul and the wall of tomes on my left, and the door, nearly covered in suit coats and academic robes hanging from so many pegs, on the right. The linguist sat behind his desk, hands locked behind his head, chair swiveled toward the couch. The robes and coats jostled as one of the professors—my mind conjures a faceless form when I try to remember which one—cracked open the door and popped his head through the crack.

Seeing me on the couch, the intruder excused himself, but the linguist asked him to continue.

"I have that media statement on family ready for you," he said.

The linguist raised an eyebrow. "Has there been a need?"

"No," the form replied.

"Good." The linguist nodded. "We'll keep it on file. But it needs to come through me," he added.

"I'll send it over."

The interaction was crisp, professional, and a bit south of neutral in a way I wouldn't have been able to pinpoint from a lineup of sinister things. Did my unconscious do the work that my sentient mind refused to process? Did I sense on any level that the school was bracing for backlash over the legalization of gay marriage just three weeks earlier in neighboring Virginia? Could I know, on any level, that this "media statement" was part and parcel of the Marriage and Family Statement that would become my undoing? From my spot on the couch in the linguist's office, the conversation was easily dismissible as university business that exceeded my pay grade. The interaction couldn't have taken more than ten seconds, but it somehow left me with the familiar feeling of dread that often lingers in the wake of those uncertain, fleeting shadows.

No, I did not have a good feeling about the conference call at all. Did Mitchell know something I didn't?

ALLISON CAME THROUGH THE FRONT door just before three o'clock the next afternoon. "Mom, everyone at work is abuzz over this whole university episode. They are dying to know what happens. They can't believe this all comes down to a *moral matter*," she said dramatically, dropping her backpack on the table and fending off Audrey, our two-year-old husky who was jumping on her in greeting.

My phone began to vibrate, so I took a deep breath and bolted to our bedroom suite, shutting the door behind me. Mitchell greeted me crisply, confirmed the presence of Dr. Raoul, and jumped right into the topic of Danny.

"It's a fine line, but an important line, to draw between hermaphrodite syndrome and someone who simply desires a sex change. I don't believe that one would apply the Marriage and Family Statement to a hermaphrodite."

I wondered why Mitchell was still using the archaic *hermaphrodite* but recognized that he correctly distinguished intersex (a visibly verifiable, medical issue) from transgender (a psychological dissonance between inward feeling and outward appearance), even though I saw those lines blurred in ways that Mitchell did not. Danny, for instance, identifies as both intersex and transgender, since he decided to transition from presenting as female to male.

The artist in me knew that rigid lines—even fine ones—make for flat, simplistic images. Realistic renderings rely on blending—a gentle back and forth smudging of colors and borders that replicate the muddling interplay of shadows and light, form and space. But more worrisome to me was Mitchell's insistence on a line at all, an all-important divider that Danny had to be on one side of or the other. Did the facts of Danny's biology allow for a tentative foothold on the right side of the line—or would he remain on the outside with everyone else who was a part of that "L ... G ... B ... T ... Q nonsense"?

"I think I'd go a bit further than calling it a fine line," I said. "The distinction is one even experts don't agree on. Some people have dualities on the chromosomal level that don't manifest physically. It's entirely possible that some people who just don't feel right in their bodies—people you might think of as 'just wanting a sex change'—could still have a biological basis for the disagreement they feel with their assigned gender. There are so many stories of people who find out in adulthood that they aren't the gender they think. The only thing I'm confident in saying is that I don't have all the answers."

I was sitting on the cold, slate platform of my tub, surveying the soap scum on the shower curtain and the husky fur tumbling across the floor. My housekeeping indiscretions kept me grounded in a tangible reality. Mitchell and Dr. Raoul were formidable, but in a vague, distant sort of way; the dirt was a force with which I could reckon. I slid down to the floor and swept my hand across the blue tile, collecting the stray fur into a ball.

"But scripture tells us God made male and female," Mitchell said, as though reminding me of a variable I'd forgotten to consider in my calculation.

"Yes, of course. But we can't ignore the scientific fact that not everyone fits with those binaries. Most of my information comes from the Intersex Society of North America, an organization devoted to public education around intersexuality. One of the most interesting facts I've found is the statistic that one in one hundred people have bodies that differ from standard male or female. If you view male and female as two ends of a continuum, these people fall at all points in between." Danny's penchant for scripts must have rubbed off on me, because I rehearsed those lines like I was auditioning for the lead in a community theater production. I had more well-rehearsed answers in my arsenal; I just needed Mitchell to feed me the right questions.

"God did not make a continuum," Mitchell said. "Scripture is clear that God made male and female. Not a continuum." There was a long pause. I imagined Dr. Raoul frowning, shaking his head, slipping Mitchell a note with scribbled points he wanted clarified. Mitchell cleared his throat and then asked, "Would you ever feel there was a time to intervene in a situation with a friend who was struggling in this area?"

"I am not really sure what you mean. Could you clarify the question?" I had no prefabricated material to address this bizarre line of questioning. I was pacing through my cavernous bathroom now as I talked, a nervous habit that serves as a tell to any observer how much I dislike phone conversations. I hate not seeing facial expressions or hand gestures—the nonverbal cues that are so important to effective communication.

"You have expressed that you don't feel called to judge, but I think scripture tells us that we are to judge. So, in your friend's case, where do you see the sin in his situation?" Mitchell said.

"What?" I exclaimed, forgetting to censor my horror. "Sin? You think that I think he sinned?"

"Well," Mitchell said, patiently, "in your friend's situation, there are, um, certain things that must be given up."

"Wait, wait, are you suggesting celibacy?"

"Yes. Yes, I am."

"I don't think that at all!" What happened to the idea of the Marriage and Family Statement not applying to a "hermaphrodite"?

At this point I could almost hear Dr. Raoul scratching furiously on an imaginary piece of scrap paper, but any actual scraping I may have heard would have been Audrey pawing at the door as Allison eavesdropped. "Tell us your thoughts on homosexuality," Mitchell asked, in apparent acknowledgment of the impasse we'd reached.

"Well, I don't believe it's a choice. It's a condition of birth. Politically I support all legislation that gives gay people equal rights." I ticked off these ideas confidently—in my mind, these were no-brainers.

"But is it wrong, in your opinion?" Mitchell was trying to elicit something more from me—something beyond a statement of policy into morality, judgment, conviction. It seemed that he really didn't care if I believed that people were born gay. He didn't even mind if I deviated left politically of university norms. He seemed to be looking for something more: explicit moral condemnation.

"The way you are born is absolutely not an issue of right and wrong," I said.

"Okay," Mitchell said, changing tracks. "Can we compare it to, say, alcoholism? Just because you are born with a proclivity toward something harmful does not mean it's okay to give into it." Mitchell seemed to be reaching deep into his own arsenal of rehearsed material, but his analogy seemed faulty to me—a logical gaffe that wouldn't hold up to scrutiny. I paused and said, simply: "Let me put it this way: if a gay Christian were to successfully live a celibate life because that was their conviction—that person is a true hero of faith. I'd like to think I could be that strong. But the truth is, I don't know that I could be. I don't know how many people are."

"But the Bible is clear that acting on such urges is an abomination."

"I am not so sure it is clear on that," I said.

"Well what would you say about verses such as ..." Mitchell's voice trailed off and became muffled in apparent consultation with Dr. Raoul. "Leviticus," he finished. "What would you say about Leviticus?"

I internally scoffed. Leviticus as a guide for modern living was a concept easily debunked. Written as ancient Jewish law—a law Christians believe was fulfilled by Christ's death and resurrection—the text prohibits things like wearing garments made of blended fabric and requires that homes with mildew be vacated until deemed clean by a priest. "Umm ... well, I would leave Leviticus completely out of the conversation," I said. "I mean, unless we're also going to talk about whether or not a priest should come and bless the fridge after the moldy leftovers have been removed. Leviticus just doesn't work in this context."

"Well one of the New Testament scriptures we can look to is 1 Corinthians," Mitchell said, as though eager to drop the Leviticus inquiry.

I knew the verses he was referencing—chapter 6, verses 9 and 10, which in many translations includes homosexuality among a list of sins that would keep one from "the kingdom of God." I also knew from talks with Tyler, paper research with Brandon, and personal study that the case was less than clear that words translated to mean modern-day homosexuality carried the same connotation in the time they were written.

I wanted to help Mitchell see that the issues we were talking about couldn't be separated from the mission of the school he served—a school that existed to train and deploy a new generation of church leaders. Shouldn't churches be on the front lines of our biggest cultural issues? Shouldn't they be scrambling to hire people equipped to help the gay teens in their youth programs? Shouldn't the next generation of church workers be so much more prepared than I was to help the Steves in their ministries? Could I, possibly, be the right person at the right time to help nudge the conversation further at this school? My failures gave me the benefit of experience with this important issue—being part of the faculty could give me an outlet to apply those lessons in a place where they could really make a difference. The church as a whole is beating a path of retreat from these issues, but it's not sustainable if churches are to remain relevant.

I fumbled through the few academic points I could recall on demand, but I realized these half-remembered arguments were not going to have any bearing at all on the outcome. Mitchell gave a weak attempt at rephrasing his "but don't you think homosexuality is wrong" question one more time, in an apparent last-ditch effort to align me in some way with the sentiments expressed in the sexuality statement. I couldn't do it. Mitchell said he was going to discuss our conversation with Dr. Raoul and Peters and that he'd be in touch.

From an interview perspective, my performance was abysmal. I threw the job away, and I knew it. Of course, I knew it going in, a fact that would seem to make illogical the anxiety that immediately set up camp in the pit of my stomach. It was no longer concern over whether I'd be hired—I'd all but accepted that I wouldn't. Rather, I worried about everything my decision implied. Publicly rejecting the Marriage and Family Statement implied that I wasn't on board with mainstream, conservative Christianity. It implied that I was, probably at that very moment, being judged, labeled, deemed unfit to teach in a Christian setting. It implied that I'd not only crossed a boundary; I'd walked right off the map. And going off the map meant, by definition, that I was lost. The prospect was terrifying.

But was wandering outside the lines more terrifying than living inauthentically every day? Than showing up at work pretending I was someone I was not—signing documents I didn't believe in, allowing the faculty and student body to think I supported an agenda that I despised? It slowly began to occur to me that my refusal to participate in evangelical Christianity's stand against its latest pet sin was about more than a job, anyway. It was no longer about figuring out the minimum acceptable answers I could give and still be hired, or the promise of a more-than-doubled salary, free tuition for everyone in my family, and the ability to pay off my house in the next couple of years. It wasn't even about having the office and the revolving door, or even about being there for those students at that school.

The fact was, I walked away from the job that quite possibly could have been the fulfillment of one of my oldest dreams over an issue that wasn't even directly *mine*. It seemed absurd that I—a happily married suburban mother— could be banned from employment over an issue of sexuality. I was baffled that I could be living a lifestyle lauded and applauded by evangelical Christianity but still deemed unfit because I didn't feel qualified to judge people who are different from me. In some ways, it would have been the easiest thing in the world to tell them what they wanted to hear, but my conscience wouldn't allow it. It wasn't just guilt over misrepresenting myself, but rather guilt over being on the wrong side of a conflict with life-and-death consequences—a war waged daily in the form of countless private battles. Invisible skirmishes that crush spirits and wound souls, struggles so deeply personal most of us never know they exist—and yet here I was, an outsider, being invited into the front lines of one person's last stand. How could I live with myself if I just walked away?

23

"What About the Lesbians in the Dorms?"

Cynthia

MY CAREER MAY HAVE DERAILED off the tenure track, but I still had two weeks' worth of semester to chug through. In fact, I had to show up in my classroom the very next day, in the aftermath of an email from Mitchell lamenting that we would not be going forward with the hiring process since we continued to "talk past each other."

"What I can't get past," Mitchell wrote, "is the idea that science and the biblical position may be at odds."

Mitchell's email confirmed to me that we *weren't* simply "talking past each other"—that his narrative of science and biblical conflict was heavily redacted, discounting times the church—not the Bible—got it wrong. The flap with Galileo over the orbit of the earth and the banning of Copernicus's seminal work come to mind. Brandon would later learn that the university drafted a similar statement decades before condemning interracial relationships. In twenty years, would they be equally embarrassed about their current denouncement of sexual minorities? It seemed likely, and I wanted to be glad I wasn't a part of it.

Not the one that got away, I reminded myself.

In the meantime, I had to figure out how to fully engage in a part of my life that was all but over. I don't remember much about being in the classroom that first day post-rejection, but I do remember the trip home in Pepito. Thanks to the magic of satellite radio, I bounced between jazz and alternative, baseball and NPR, with frequent detours into pop and house music on my commutes, adjusting the programming to match my mood. My first teaching night after being fired (because, honestly, that's what it was; I hadn't seen it yet, but an email had been sent to adjuncts that afternoon requiring everyone to "affirm the statement" in writing as a condition of continued employment) quickly became an NPR night.

The topic was LGBTQ—and I'll just stop here to add in the "I" that so irks Danny when omitted—youth suicide rates. Caller after caller phoned in with stories that successively amped my outrage: parents who felt like they had to choose between their children and their faith; churches that shunned families for standing by gay daughters and sons; kids who ran away to avoid the shame. It's like the issue somehow followed me from campus and insisted on riding shotgun. I'll never know if the actual transcript of the show would support my impression, but the message to my ears was a resounding: "If someone had been there, this tragedy could have been averted." Instead, stories that should have been about faith communities rallying around hurting people were now fodder for call-in shows, blow-by-blows about how the church abandoned them.

I spent that commute awash in frustration and loss over what could have been. So much of me wished I could have found a way into the undercover agent role—someone who would create an unexpected safe space for closeted students. I didn't know which students on campus were gay, but statistics and rumors made me confident they were there. How different things might have been for them had I been able to stay, if I'd had an office that served as a stop on something akin to a queer underground railroad. What would become of those students now, whoever they were?

Everything raged the next day: the sky, my fingers across my keyboard, my texts to Joanna. I wanted words to purge my feelings of loss—not just mine, but of our broader, fractured faith community that seemed to be more interested in creating rules than room. I camped out on my couch with a bottomless mug of coffee, my keyboard, and Audrey, pounding out what became an open letter to my students that I resolved to post right after I submitted my final grades. Until then, I determined to keep the issue as far away from my classroom as possible.

My last day on campus, three of my students asked me why I wasn't returning for the spring semester. I told them the truth. The responses summarized the problem better than I ever could.

Yolanda, a nineteen-year-old single mother: "What? But there are lesbians in the dorms!"

The younger of a pair of perpetually skirt-clad, far-right, rural, conservative sisters: "I don't understand what that has to do with you teaching English."

A thirtysomething Black woman who went by the single letter "T," for whom my class was her first-ever foray into higher education: "I hope they don't find out about me."

24

Questions

Cynthia

"My parents are no longer okay with me. They want to meet with me alone. They don't understand why I can't just live as a girl. They seem hurt and disappointed."

The text came in from Danny moments before I expected him to walk through my door. After the successful talk with his family days earlier, he decided the next step was to share his news with a few of his closer church friends before a meeting the coming Sunday when he planned to tell the others in church leadership. Only now we had the twofold problem of this potential reversal of his parents' support and the fact that the group of friends he was going to talk with before Sunday were filling dinner plates in my kitchen while they waited for him to arrive.

Edward, a pharmacist, and Andi, an elementary school teacher, were part of a small group that met at our house on Monday evenings to share a meal, our lives, and thoughts about various Bible topics. We considered them to be among our closer friends, and they played a unique role in our lives. They were Brandon's older friends (Brandon was in a band with Edward and Pastor Dave's son Matt) and our younger friends. Andi and I had known each other briefly twelve years earlier, lost touch, and reconnected when our family joined the Inlet. She wore quirky patterned clothes and thick black glasses that gave her a sort of bespectacled Zooey Deschanel *New Girl* look.

Edward was blond and lanky and tended toward a brand of dry, witty banter that served as a sort of conversational playground.

Danny was close with these people, too, even though he wasn't a regular for Monday dinner. But he'd asked to come that night so he could share his story specifically with these friends.

"Okay, so what's this meeting about Sunday?" Edward said, settling into our sectional sofa next to Andi. "I mean, you know, don't you?"

Now I found myself in the uncomfortable position of fielding Edward's barrage of questions. "We're going to know eventually," he said. "So why not just tell us what's going on?"

"It's just not that simple," I said.

"Okay, so you can just say yes or no, then. Is someone gay?"

"No, Edward, no one is gay."

"How about Dani and Joanna? Is this about them?" Edward pressed and I squirmed a bit too long.

"Okay so it's about Dani and Joanna. They want to tell us that they're gay."

Things would have been so much simpler if that were true, if I could just say, "Yes, Edward, Dani and Joanna are gay." I knew that's what Andi already thought. One evening Joanna had come to our weekly gathering and a visitor had been there who said something insensitive about homosexuality. Andi cringed recalling the moment after the visitor left, "Because, you know, Joanna..."

"Okay, now we're getting somewhere!" Edward said. "Dani and Joanna are gay."

I grabbed my phone, thumbs tapping out an SOS to Danny. "Edward won't stop asking questions! What do you want me to say?" There was no chance I'd divulge Danny's story but also no chance Edward's pestering would subside. I hit send and hoped for a reply.

My phone lit up. "I'm with Elaine now. I'll stop by on my way to my parents."

I was shocked that he wanted to deal with this now on top of everything else, but he had to. He wanted—needed—to shape his story. To control the narrative.

I looked up from my phone. "Danny is on the way. Your questions will be answered," I said, dodging the need to use a pronoun.

"But you can't give us a preview?" Edward pushed.

"No! It's not my story to tell."

In fairness, Andi and Edward weren't just nosy parishioners. They each had history with Danny that went back way further than the couple of weeks since Danny and I became friends. In a different church almost a decade and a half earlier, Andi and Edward had both been teen members of Danny and Joanna's youth group. Knowing firsthand the deep nature of those relationships, I felt uneasy about being the one in the know while they sat wondering what was going on with their former mentor.

Brad managed to steer the conversation toward our study topic for the evening.

Danny finally showed up at the door and sank, once again, into what was becoming his spot on my blue sectional. He took a deep breath and launched into the latest rendition of his script. He still took frequent breaks to clear his throat—a habit I was beginning to identify as a verbal tic—but he stumbled less and actually managed eye contact.

When he finished, he looked straight at Andi and Edward. "Do you have any questions?"

"I am just disappointed that you never felt like you could tell us," Andi said.

"I didn't tell anyone." His voice was patient and gentle.

Andi and Edward shook their heads. "No," Andi said. "No questions."

If Danny registered the unconvincing tone, he ignored it, heading to the door with a promise to return after he left his parents' house.

"So, is she saying she has man parts?" Edward said, as soon as the door closed. He and Andi both wore uncomfortable expressions. They definitely were not without questions.

"Intersex means you have both," I said.

"So, she has lady parts," Edward said.

"Yes," I said, slowly.

"So, she's still a woman."

"Biologically both," I said, before blurting in exasperation, "Edward, you are a doctor!"

"But we learned systems," he said. "I didn't really learn the parts."

I narrowed my eyes and scrunched my nose, shaking my head. This was classic Edward: a high school sophomore with a lab coat. Most of the time it was charming, but tonight I was simply baffled.

Brad stepped in and attempted to explain it all again, and I realized in amusement that he was developing a script too.

"But she wasn't truthful," Andi said. "She lied to us all those years."

"But it wasn't about you, Andi. It was about him. It isn't a reflection on your relationship."

Andi gathered her books and reached for her bag.

"Are you okay?" I asked.

"I'm just sad that she didn't feel she could just tell us." Andi rose from my sofa and Edward followed her to the door.

25

Free

Danny

My stomach hurt in all the same places it had days earlier. Same clammy hands, same tightness in my throat.

Is acceptance too much to hope for, after all? What changed since I left here the other day, finally feeling like myself?

I glanced at my mother as I entered the house, surprised not to see anger on her face, but something else entirely: fear. *What is Mom afraid of?*

"I've been doing some research since you left. And I have questions."

Her voice was soft, but that did nothing to quiet my heart as it thumped in my chest. Questions could be good … or terrible.

"I just want to know what you're doing with your past."

"My past? What do you mean, Mom?"

"Do I have to hide all the pictures?"

Relief and sympathy flooded through me. "No!" I was emphatic. "My past is my past. It brought me to where I am today."

Mom seemed relieved, but worry flashed across her face again. "I was there," she said, "when you were born. You were a girl." Mom wasn't combative or angry—she looked genuinely confused.

I took a deep breath and went over it all again, explaining things and reassuring her until she seemed okay again.

I got back in my car and headed straight for Cynthia and Brad's house to debrief. I always felt better processing things out loud with them. They were good sounding boards. As I navigated the short drive, I started processing the conversation with my mom. *That's the problem with being both,* I thought. I lived more than forty years as a girl and then a woman—that experience was my *life*: I couldn't change it, and I didn't want to. Even now, eager as I was to go forward as myself—the grown-up version of the little boy I'd also always been inside—I didn't want to lose my past or my present. And, looking back, my mother didn't want to either.

❧

BY THE TIME SUNDAY CAME, I realized I was getting used to feeling nervous. This after-church meeting was the first time telling my story to a group that included near strangers, some of whom had the power to yank something important from my life—the youth group. I scanned the room for friendly faces. Elaine was near the exit with a couple of the youth group parents. Cynthia and Brad were seated across the room.

Pastor Dave said something about bringing everyone together to discuss a medical issue someone was having. That's what he told me he'd say. I also knew he'd prepped several of the people in the room, and very few people here had come in blind. Still, my heart pounded as Dave said a prayer, and then suddenly, about fifteen pairs of eyes were on me.

I inhaled a big, shaky breath and then went straight into my script. I felt a little more confident this time—I guess practice does that.

"The most important thing I want you all to know is that I'm still me. I'm still Dani—I'm just swapping the *i* for a *y*," I joked. I barely had time to catch my breath before people began jumping in with support.

Ted, one of the NASA scientists, jumped in with facts about how prevalent being intersex is. I felt myself begin to breathe again. Ted was someone who really worried me. He was probably the most conservative member of the Inlet, and he had strong opinions about almost everything.

Ted barely finished his thought before Nolan, a physicist, broke in. "It's as common as red hair," he said, going on to recount a story about a woman who was stunned to be denied a marriage license after her blood test results revealed that she was genetically male.

Androgen insensitivity syndrome, I thought. Nolan didn't call it by name, but I wouldn't have been able to until recently either.

Even Chet, the wildcard vocalist who quit service mid-song as often as not, chimed in with some tidbit from an EMT course he once took.

The meeting was going better than I could have dreamed.

And then, suddenly, Bill, another NASA guy, a physicist with a gray, bushy beard and wild eyes that blinked sparingly behind thick, round glasses, shook his head rather ominously. "We need to be prepared," he said. "In about six weeks, things are going to get pretty noisy around here."

"You think? How so?" Pastor Dave's voice hit its upper registers in surprise.

Bill stroked his beard and nodded. "Oh, yes. Once the media gets ahold of this, things are going to get noisy for a while."

I was equally bewildered and alarmed.

Holy cow! The media? How would they even know?

I shot a look at Cynthia, who I could see was suppressing laughter as she shook her head from side to side. I glanced at Elaine, who mirrored Cynthia's expression. I pressed my lips together to avoid reaction.

"Let's pray!" Bill's wife, Maude, jumped in with the suggestion. Since I was seated mid-circle, Maude, a plump, retired biology professor, gathered everyone around me. She placed a hand on my shoulder and began to pray. She started strong, affirming my courage and asking for blessing and wisdom, but began to falter when it came time to use a pronoun. "Please help ummm, him—um, her ..." she began to trail. She plowed forward, bungling my pronouns. Cynthia corrected her a few times, and then she mercifully said, "Amen."

And that was it. The meeting, although awkward, had ended without incident, and I was now just a couple steps away from being fully out. I'd shared the news with my family, close friends, and church leadership. I had registered my change of status with my company's HR department, running into nothing more than a tongue-in-cheek quip that I'd just messed up her "women in management numbers." Each positive interaction had given me the boost I needed to go another step. Now I was ready to go public.

The following Sunday, the congregation formed a circle around the sanctuary for the Lord's Prayer, and I readied myself to come out again, for the penultimate time. This was it: I was going to be fully out in my church community: an intersex youth pastor: out, male, and in ministry. I stood on the threshold of a dream that had seemed unapproachable my entire life. The moment was huge, but this time I felt more confident sharing my story. Around that prayer circle I saw my support system—people who already knew, people who wouldn't let this go wrong. I took a breath and plunged into a fresh recitation of my script. When I stopped speaking, I realized I was surrounded by words of affirmation and hugs. Pastor Dave prayed, and the group responded with a smattering of "amens"—except for Elaine, who was beaming as she shouted: "I prepared you so well for this!"

This rendition of my script ended in a plea for questions: good ones, bad ones, I didn't care. I was fully aware that inquiries would spring from a range of sources: curiosity, misinformation, or, worst case, bigotry. But I wanted to be an approachable source of factual information—someone who could demystify a population that seldom gets the chance I had to be welcomed in a church. I hung back afterward, giving and receiving hugs, fielding basic, unmemorable questions—happy to do anything I could to make this easier for someone else later on. I left the Inlet and headed home to take the final step forward into the life I had never thought attainable: my own.

I STARED AT MY REFLECTION looking back at me on my phone. This was it. I'd hit record, recite my script a final time, and it would be done. The quickest way I knew to come out publicly was through social media, so in a final burst of courage I recorded a simple, digital explanation: intersex, my inability to continue presenting the female image people expected to see, how I was still the same person. Adding, as I had at the Inlet, an invitation for questions and conversations. I kept it short and to the point.

As I hit post and sent the video into cyberspace, I thought about the people who would see it. My parents' friends. Acquaintances from old churches. People from college. Jen, the middle school mean girl who, as an adult, was actually rather nice. Former youth group members. And, with a pang of sadness, I thought of someone who deserved to see it but never would: Tess. Tess, my old friend and Megan's sister, who had come out as a lesbian in her late teens and was judged by everyone—even me—and then died of breast cancer years before I could apologize or explain myself to her.

A lot of support came in that day, but when my phone pinged and I saw her name, I knew this was the person I'd been waiting to hear from: Megan. Happily married Megan who, all these years later, still occupied a bittersweet place in my heart. Through tears, I read her apologies for the past and encouragement for my future, and just like that, one of my oldest wounds closed. The video was my peace with my past. Viewers could decide if they wanted to follow me into the future. Because that's where I was headed. I was free. Free to be me, anywhere. Everywhere. All the time.

26

The Net Is Fraying

Cynthia

MY PHONE LIT UP WITH a message from Joanna. "I want to talk to you about what's going on with Danny and me, but not over text."

I was sad and frustrated that their future was in question, and I told her so.

"Me too." I watched the trio of gray bubbles dancing on my screen as I waited for her to continue. "And let me tell you how happy it makes me to be able to talk to a friend about my marriage!" Her text ended in a string of exclamation points.

Marriage. The word was out—what a relief it must be, I thought. I remembered how Elaine had said Danny and Joanna weren't a couple, and I took the text I was staring at as proof positive that she was wrong. But the word *marriage* also fanned my growing frustration with Danny. Why wasn't he excited to finally be open about the marriage that was his too? It didn't make sense to me that things would fall apart between them now. Surely Danny wouldn't leave Joanna just at the moment when they could finally live publicly as a couple—after twenty-six years. It seemed incomprehensible to me. I hated the thought of the relationship falling apart just when it seemed, from my vantage point, to have its best chance at success.

Part of my investment in their relationship was selfish. Danny and Joanna were jointly part of the community that had built up around me during a time I desperately needed a snapshot of my own future. When I first came to the Inlet, I had only recently stopped lying on my bathroom floor, tallying the hairs I'd collected as they fell from my head each day, praying the number would be less than one hundred: the threshold, copious websites agreed, for normal shedding. But the count seldom fell below triple digits, and I was losing my sanity faster than my hair. That was the year I stopped teaching art, the year our family dogs died, the year I purchased Groupons obsessively as boredom insurance. My kids were on the threshold of leaving for the first time and it was hard, then, to see anything meaningful ahead.

Even though my hair eventually went back to normal (doctors chalked it up to stress or a fluke), even though I was happily teaching at Christopher Newport and had already adopted my husky puppy, life still felt a little raw, a little lonely. Then came the Inlet—another one of those places that, for me, became an instant home. Even before I heard Pastor Dave emphasize the importance of living in community—it's how we're designed, it's how we're wired, he'd tell us—I felt it there, inside those doors. And I stumbled into that place at a moment when community was the very thing I craved.

Lines of connection began to form between Brad and me and other people, other events. Those lines quickly became a web—a safety net. The Inlet, Elaine, Andi and Edward, Pastor Dave and his wife, Joanna, and now Danny, became the net that held me in those months after I crawled back from my psychological abyss. Sure, I was doing a lot better then, especially with the kids back home (Allison between apartments and Brandon on the weekends), but that was temporary. And now, with not only my tenure-track promotion gone but the entire Bible college gig along with it, loss still seemed to be looming on the periphery of my life. I needed that net to stay intact.

But Danny and Joanna's relationship wasn't the only weak point. Looking back, I can see the places where the holes first began to widen—the early signs of unraveling that were easy to ignore.

The first time I caught myself waving off misgivings was during the conversation I had with Danny the night he came back to my house to debrief after the not-so-great Monday dinner conversation with Edward and Andi.

"How do you think it went with them?"

I hedged. "They can't get over the idea that you kept it from them. I think they feel hurt."

"I didn't tell anyone!"

"I think they were taken aback. They'll come around in time."

And I believed it. For the first time in my adult life, I felt I was experiencing *true* Christianity at the Inlet—life lived out among a community: Black and white, doctors and addicts, comfortable and homeless; there was a place for everyone. The Inlet was the exception to all those church lessons I internalized; at the Inlet it was okay to disagree or experience life differently, and no one would leave, right?

Pastor Dave frequently reminded us that everyone had something to offer—that *all* were welcome. Conservative views had their place at the Inlet too—but not intolerance. I had no doubt that this congregation was going to demonstrate that, regardless of what the university believed, a matter of biology would pose no threat to our commitment to Christ or to each other. We would prove that the church can be a place for open dialogue, a place where faith and science could peacefully thrive. I couldn't wait to watch it happen. Andi and Edward had been a part of the community for much longer than we had. They knew what the Inlet was all about. They'd come around—I knew it.

But then the following Sunday, Andi and Edward quietly slipped out after service instead of joining the small group that gathered in the little side room to meet with Danny. Then they began making excuses not to come to our standing Monday meal. Pastor Dave's son Matt, who had also been a young adult leader in one of Danny and Joanna's youth groups, joined his friends Andi and Edward in feeling personally duped. And just days after the meeting at the Inlet, Pastor Dave himself surfaced with his own doubts.

"If Danny is a man, then what has he been doing with Joanna all these years?" he asked Brad over the phone one evening. Explanations of their clandestine marriage didn't help Pastor Dave or the plethora of other Inlet members who began asking similar questions. People wanted to know where things stood with them currently.

I didn't know then that the magnifying glass aimed at this right-now moment in Danny's life warped our perspective. I didn't understand that Joanna's apparent investment in her relationship with Danny represented a brand-new hole in our fraying net. I didn't know Danny had initially reached out to Elaine because he was trying to find a path toward a new, independent life. I had no idea that the summer before the grilled portobellos, Krista—the former youth group student turned friend—had pulled Danny back from falling into an abyss of his own.

27
Physical Realities

Cynthia

SUNDAY LUNCH WAS BECOMING ONE of those constants I looked forward to. We'd usually join Danny and Joanna, one or both of our kids, Rob the Customer, and a couple teens from youth group around a table at one of our preapproved restaurants. Danny and I were weak links in our culinary club—Danny's soy allergy and my aversion to meat narrowed our options, making pizza joints and Mexican places hot spots.

A few weeks after Danny posted his coming-out video, several of us were standing around in the church parking lot trying to determine whether it was a Mexican or pizza day when Danny suddenly pulled a card from his wallet and held it next to his face. "Check this out, guys," he said.

We took turns squinting at the photo on Danny's work ID card. The visual evidence was stunning, something I never would have believed had I not seen it in laminate plastic and flesh and blood in front of me. Danny's haircut—a genuine, barber-issued, male haircut—was an obvious, explainable change. It was the evolution of Danny's facial structure that was shocking. He hadn't lost a bit of weight, yet the softness in his face had been replaced by more chiseled, squarish features.

We gaped in shock at the transformation. Much in the way that parents cannot detect the continuous, microscopic changes in their infants until they accumulate over days or weeks, we had failed to see the myriad ways Danny was morphing before our eyes.

Danny laughed. New Danny did that a lot.

"That's not all!" Danny's eyes flashed as he ran a hand up his bare leg to emphasize a layer of thick, masculine hair.

"Wait, wait," I said, "This just *happened*? You haven't done anything?" I knew the answer to this question already. Danny planned to begin taking testosterone but he had a long series of appointments to go through first. Still, visible, physical changes couldn't just magically happen—could they?

"Nope," Danny said. "I haven't taken a thing. This is just my body, on its own."

It's hard to say if the evidence spoke more to the burden of stress or the power of the mind, but either way, Danny's body was syncing up with his brain to cast a unified vote on the issue of his gender: male, by a landslide.

The visual confirmation of Danny's transformation was my introduction to the myriad physical issues that specifically intersex, but potentially other nonbinary people, experience. In Danny's case, the changes—the amplification of masculine features—were welcome ones. Danny had told me about how his female organs had shut down and led to his hysterectomy, but that kind of made sense to me; it seemed to compute.

I didn't realize then how much was at stake for Danny physically, but it wasn't long until I began to understand how little I knew. One Saturday morning, I made the two-block trek from my house to the Inlet to drop off a cup of coffee for Brandon, who was in the middle of rehearsal for Sunday's song service. Danny was there, too, with a bulging lip packed with cotton.

"What happened?" I asked.

I parsed through Danny's muffled narrative to learn that he'd bitten into something at work the day before and his tooth gave way, shifting precariously across a gumline that was suddenly and unsettlingly soft.

My face must have registered my shock, but Danny shrugged it off. "Hormones," he managed in garbled tones. "Dental problems are really common with intersex people."

"Just wait until he hits second adolescence," Joanna jumped into the conversation from across the room.

"Second adolescence?"

"Oh yeah," she said. "Once his hormones get regulated, it will be like he's a teenager all over again. You need to know these things." Joanna laughed.

In committing to be a vocal ally, I knew I'd signed up for a lot of research. Accordingly, I'd been scouring my university's databases in an effort to make sense of what was happening to me in a cultural and moral sense, as well as what was happening to Danny physically. But seeing Danny's cotton-packed mouth was not just a shock; it was also an indication of how little I truly understood about the physical impact of being intersex. I wanted to know more about the physical realities of Danny's story and the spiritual and moral backbone of mine.

My research soon led me to the story of someone who embodied *both* of our situations. A professor I will call Dr. C. taught theology at Azusa Pacific University, a private Christian university in Southern California. Dr. C taught for fifteen years, serving for a time as department chair. But by 2012 she had become seriously ill with an undiagnosed malady. Her weight dipped dangerously low, her organs were failing, and doctors, family, friends, colleagues, and Dr. C. herself understood the inevitable: she was dying. She made out her will and began saying her goodbyes to family and friends.

At some point, a new doctor ended up reviewing Dr. C.'s case and asked the one question no one else had broached: Why was she taking hormones and psychiatric drugs? The doctor then learned that Dr. C. had been prescribed the medications as part of a decades-long and increasingly desperate bid to remain the woman, wife, mother, and Christian professional everyone expected her to be.

"But do you identify as a woman?" the doctor asked.

"No, absolutely not." Like Danny, Dr. C. had always assumed she'd grow up to be a boy. What happened instead was female puberty, an acceptance of Christian faith, and a desire for ministry and family. After the failure of a first marriage, Dr. C. doubled down her efforts and tried everything she could think of to become a model Christian woman. Medical doctors prescribed hormones and psychiatrists wrote prescriptions for mental illness. But this new doctor told her she wasn't a crazy woman but a transgender man. His treatment plan was simple: stop taking everything. And with that, Dr. C. was reborn—as the man I met: Heath Adam Ackley.

Once Ackley's body took over, two things happened: he returned to full health, and he began to look much more masculine. So masculine that he knew he'd have to bring his students and employers into what was happening. His students, who had mostly figured it out, were affirming and supportive; his administration, less so. I read so many articles about the factors and forces behind Ackley's interaction with Azusa, but the fact that mattered to me— the one that caused me to find and message him through social media—was the end result: within days after informing HR of his impending name change, he was pulled from the classroom.

Ackley stood at the intersection of both my experiences and Danny's in such a specific, dead-center way that I knew I had to meet him. After exchanging a few DMs on Twitter, we made plans for a virtual chat.

The person who popped up on my MacBook screen was unrecognizable from the blonde soccer-mom image of Dr. C that I'd seen during my research. The Ackley talking with me from his backyard in California sported salt-and-pepper facial hair and clutched a pipe—professorial almost to a fault.

"Thank you for what you are doing," Adam said. "You aren't alone." He began ticking off instances he knew of where straight, Christian allies experienced everything from job loss to death threats. There he stopped. "You need to be prepared for that." He shot off the name of an author. "Reach out to her. Tell her I sent you. She can help prepare you for the death threats."

I should have been alarmed, but at that moment, I felt relief. I hadn't yet learned how to talk about my writing and sensed a lot of skepticism when I tried to talk about it. I'd spent weeks feeling that my story was a weak echo co-opting the problems of another demographic. And now, here was Adam, telling me my role as a Christian ally was so dangerous, so key, it could lead to death threats.

"Not everyone speaks out," Adam said. "And I get that. I know a lot of allies in Christian jobs who remain silent because they need those jobs."

I could have taken that stance. It was an option part of me wished I'd taken. I certainly didn't think of myself as someone who "didn't need" a good job offer.

"What happened to you is called ally discrimination."

It had a name. For me, a writer, that made what happened more real than even living through it. Names made things real. Names gave you something to write down, see, underscore.

Adam took a pull on his pipe and then began telling me live, in real time, sentiments I'd seen quoted in many articles about him: the hurt and disappointment of discovering his long-term colleagues preferred him as a mentally-ill, dying woman over a healthy transgender man.

And there was the answer to the question that popped up from time to time in the dark corners of my mind: why I couldn't be one of the silent—the people who cash a paycheck while checking their inner selves at the door. I couldn't be a part of the inhumanity of preferring someone's suffering, even someone's death, over a remedy that simply challenged established belief systems.

Adam and I talked for over an hour. Among other things, he helped solidify an idea that Danny and I had discussed many times: that intersex and trans aren't independent concepts but a part of a bigger picture that researchers are still working to understand. Adam maintains that variations in a handful of gender markers (neurological, hormonal, chromosomal factors, for instance) impact gender identity, making biology perhaps the strongest determining factor in whether or not someone is transgender. I left that conversation feeling affirmed, both in my role as an ally and in my grasp of the issues.

In Danny's dental crisis, I became an eyewitness to the physical realities of a condition that my colleagues—and Adam's— were quick to write off as moral shortcomings. I was shocked that universities, places designed to seek truth, were so afraid that a scientific reality might clash with their perception of a spiritual concept that they refused to examine it. Even though that type of interrogation could be frightening, might scare off donors, and would almost certainly shift long-held assumptions, what use is a university that makes decisions on fear rather than fact?

But my church, I knew, would do better. For me, the Inlet was a place from which I could embrace inquiry and investigation and remain solidly grounded in a spiritual community. It comforted me to belong to a church that allowed religion and reason to wrestle in ways that strengthened and sharpened our understanding of both.

28

Severed Connections

Cynthia

"Do you use words like *divorce*?"

"I thought, I mean ..." Danny's voice trailed. "I didn't think there was any confusion."

Ugh, I thought, momentarily convinced that Danny had become so thoroughly male he was now in some sort of stereotypical Mars-Venus communication gaffe with Joanna. "I just don't understand why you are leaving her now after all this time," I said.

"We haven't slept in the same room in years," Danny said.

"But what about Joanna's post last summer when you killed the bug in the night?"

Danny forced air through his lips in frustration. "I was shocked when I saw that post. I came from my room on the second floor—where I moved years ago. She screamed so loud it woke me."

"But the marriage..."

"It's been over for years. It's true I took her with me to Europe last summer—it was a last-ditch attempt to rekindle things. We had a great time, but it was only as friends. She hasn't been interested in me in a long time." Danny paused. "But she has been interested in other people. We haven't lived as a couple in a long time."

Danny's big news that evening, after he'd settled into his spot on my sectional and modeled a new pair of boat shoes, was an announcement of his intention to find a place to live on his own, without Joanna.

On one hand I was beginning to realize that Danny's version of his life with Joanna differed significantly from Joanna's account of their union. On the other, I wondered how much the past mattered since Joanna seemed so invested in Danny's life right now. Shouldn't he be willing to give their marriage a chance?

"She is always going to be in my life. It's kind of a thing in the trans community—exes are family. There's an understanding that we go through a lot with our partners," he said. "Whoever I eventually date will need to know that."

I paused, realizing that up to that point, my view of Danny and Joanna's relationship had come from a single source: Joanna. I remembered Elaine's insistence that they weren't a couple the night Danny talked with his family. I recalled Joanna's tears and sullen demeanor, talking with Elaine before Danny arrived. It suddenly seemed not only possible, but probable, that Joanna's version of the story wasn't the definitive account.

"Joanna is important to me," Danny was saying, with nothing but care and compassion in his voice. "But she's become more like a sister to me, and I need her to accept that. Can you help me here? Like when she starts talking this way, can you try to reinforce the idea of me in a brotherly role? Let's call it Project Sibling."

I laughed at the prospect of embarking on a named mission with Danny, even as I knew brother Danny would be a tough sell. Yes, I told Danny. I'll try. Project Sibling.

DAYS LATER, JOANNA STARTED TALKING about Danny in a way that suggested a future wildly different from what one might have with a sibling, and I hedged. "What will you do if things don't work out that way?"

"What do you mean?"

"Talking with him the other night, I just think, well..."

Joanna tensed, and I scrambled for appropriate things to say. Project Sibling had a clearly defined mission, but no policies, no scripts. I was on my own.

Suddenly, Joanna laughed. "Wait, wait," she said, relief bathing her voice, her face, her posture. "You talked with Danny before Sunday, didn't you?"

"Yeah, Thursday, actually."

Joanna nodded as her lips pressed together and her eyes crinkled in amusement. "We had a fight, but we worked it all out. We're good now! Wow, you had me worried for a moment," she said, laughing.

Some part of me realized how unlikely it was that Danny and Joanna had a Sunday reckoning that rebuilt everything, but in the moment, I allowed myself to join in Joanna's relief.

⸻

"So," DANNY SAID, SETTLING INTO my sofa one night the following week. "Any update on Project Sibling?" Behind his black rectangular glasses I saw amusement flicker in his eyes at the mention of our mission code name.

"I... thought it might be off?"

"Off? Why?" Danny's eyes widened. "Project Sibling is definitely not off." His voice hit what was possibly the lowest register I'd heard from him.

Danny scoffed and sputtered at the account I offered of my conversation with Joanna. If that moment was a red flag, then the text I woke up to the next morning was a full-scale drill: flashing lights, alarms, sirens.

JOANNA: Do you have anything earth-shattering to tell me about my life today?

ME: No?

JOANNA: Well, since you were with Danny last night I thought I'd better check LOL.

I cringed. LOLs and emojis were classic Joanna deflectors. Text-speak was a sure sign she wasn't laughing out loud. I realized then that she was fishing—wondering what Danny told me, feeling out what I knew.

⸙

THE BARRAGE OF QUESTIONS CONTINUED as I sat next to Joanna on a cheaply upholstered chair in a nondescript waiting room. I'd gone with her to a doctor's appointment and listened while she fumed. "He's in or he's out," she said. "And I don't think he realizes what *out* means. He won't be in our lives. When Momma dies, he won't be at her funeral. He has until the end of this month to decide."

The Danny Joanna described—fickle, dodging commitment—was hard to reconcile with the Danny desperate to exit a loveless living situation. Looking back, I don't wonder how I decided who to believe, which of my two friends to trust, to stand by, when it became clear that Danny and Joanna remaining family was an impossible ideal. Of course, the narrative had two versions: two alternate story lines, two trajectories. As a writer, the concept of multiple perspectives is basic to my thinking. But my instincts drew me toward the story that was more inclusive, minus hard lines and barriers—the story that always continued with Danny saying, "She needs you. Don't give up on her."

Joanna's narrative was punctuated with ultimatums: emphasis on alliances, deadlines, and debts. Danny focused on the possibilities for the future, while Joanna clung to a varnished version of the past, editing out the chapters that unfolded on separate floors, in separate beds. Danny's story would be the one that resonated, the one I wanted to align with. Meanwhile, Joanna began to gather the frayed ends of our unraveling network and twist them into a cord—her lifeline. Our friendship wasn't the only thing beginning to disintegrate; it was just falling apart the fastest.

⸙

THE FURNITURE WAS STILL SCRAPING overhead when I heard the unmistakable thump of our porch screen door as Brandon and Danny returned from dinner at our usual Mexican place.

"We'll never be able to go back," Danny was saying as the signature gasping giggle of Brandon's laughter filled the house. It was a sound I loved and, combined with the thumping above, filled me with a sense of joy and completeness. I tend to be at my happiest when my house is at its loudest.

"The waiter's face," Brandon sputtered as he followed Danny through the dining room, into the kitchen.

"The waiter," Danny said, entering the room, "not our usual one, ma'amed me, like, what, three, four times?" he looked at Brandon for verification.

Being called ma'am in public was a sore point with Danny, a still-too-common occurrence that I'd never seen elicit amusement, let alone hysterics.

Between their gasping fits of laughter and asides, I parsed out the punchline. Despite numerous corrections, the waiter persisted in calling Danny ma'am—right up to the moment he delivered the check. Danny pulled a card from his wallet and slammed it on the table, but it wasn't until he saw the confusion wash over the waiter's face that he realized the card he actually presented was a plastic "man card" he slid into his wallet after receiving it as a gag gift over the holidays.

The laughter summoned Allison halfway down the staircase running along the front wall of our kitchen. "Almost ready up here!" she said.

While the guys were at dinner, she'd shoved her personal belongings to the back of her bedroom in makeshift storage, opening up the rest of the space for Danny. Because, in the end, Danny hadn't decided to move out of Joanna's house—she'd asked him to leave.

Elaine drafted a DIY, unofficial, nonbinding divorce agreement, and because Danny was almost maddingly determined not to say anything disparaging about Joanna, and he still took financial responsibility for her household for Momma Miller's sake, he would be sending most of his paycheck to Joanna—leaving Allison's recently vacated, half-empty bedroom as his best option for a new address. I worried a bit about giving him half a room, wondering if we needed to do a more thorough reorganization of our second floor. But Danny said it would be temporary—just a few weeks until he got on his feet and figured something out.

A couple weeks after he'd settled in, Danny announced he wanted to start dating. A few days later, he was more specific. "I think I want to start dating Krista," he said. "I want to ask her to be my girlfriend."

Krista, now graduated from college, had just returned to Hampton Roads, and Danny, despite the age difference, despite the roles he'd played in her past—female-presenting youth leader, pseudo-landlord, boss, and friend—now wanted to see if she'd accept him as his authentic self in the form of a fully male boyfriend. And it wasn't too many days after he'd made that announcement that our family seemed to expand again as Krista joined us.

That summer, Danny operated in one of three basic states: working, sleeping, or corralling us for dinner, drinks, or outings. There were good days and bad days as Danny ticked off milestones: his official name change, getting hormone therapy, and obtaining a new driver's license, passport, and credit cards. I immediately knew which category each day fell into for Danny as soon as he opened the door each evening. If it was a good day, I'd hear Danny's voice calling out a hearty, "Hola!" right after the keypad beeped. It was always Spanish on good days. Bad days were heavy, palpable. Danny still greeted us through the cloud, but never in Spanish.

Danny's usual mode was upbeat; as a housemate he rolled with the punches. He was usually the first person to jump in when something went wrong—like the Sunday afternoon I discovered that the pantry had been infiltrated by an unwelcome guest. Danny was the first person to reach into the pantry and grab some canned goods to start the unloading effort.

I also enjoyed watching Danny's friendship with Brad start to truly bloom. They'd go to the movies together sometimes on Friday afternoons, when Danny's company would rent out a movie theater. Krista and I thought it was totally adorable that Danny always chose Brad for his plus-one on those outings. One movie day, Brad was supposed to pick up Danny and another guy at Danny's office, but his car broke down. Since the only other vehicle available was Danny's smart car, Brad feared movie day was going to be a bust. As Brad likes to tell it, "We had three guys and a smart car, but I called Danny and he said, 'I got this.' And he did." Danny came to get Brad on time in a rental—that he somehow scored for free.

But although Danny could be the life of the party, when he shut down, he was out—sometimes for a very long time.

One late Saturday afternoon, I got a text from Krista. "I know this is going to sound weird, but is Danny in the house? We were supposed to have plans today, but I haven't heard from him in twenty-four hours."

Alarmed, I alerted Brad, and we ran upstairs. We thought Danny was with Krista. We banged on the door and heard a groggy voice. He was alive. About ten minutes later we all got a text from upstairs: Danny was taking us all out for dinner. "Sorry for the scare!"

Danny also developed a love for Axe body spray. A week into airing fumes from the kitchen after he left for work, I realized it was a drill I'd been through before—with Brandon as a younger teen. I remembered the potent body spray as a ubiquitous rite of teen guy passage and the pieces fell into place. Day-long Saturday naps, late nights, and Axe baths: it was second adolescence—and this one, arguably, a bigger milestone than the first.

⌁

IN HAITI, ONCE, I WATCHED a weathered, middle-aged man crouching with a spool of white string: an endless line of cord passing through his calloused hands and transformed into an expanse of framed open spaces—a fishing net. The work was flawless, pristine—a skill passed down through generations of island families who rely on nets to gather, secure, and contain the sea bounty they eat and sell. But even the most well-constructed net is just a piece of loosely woven fabric: interlocking stitches secured at points of intersection. And no fabric is immune to repeated use or damage; no material lasts forever. Connections sever, holes widen, and nets weaken—whether made of rope, string, plastic, or, in the case of the personal safety net unwinding beneath me, flesh-and-blood humans, themselves only as strong as their own support systems.

When Krista said yes to Danny, he gained a girlfriend, I gained a friend, and the Inlet, collectively, gained a reason to question Danny's motives.

Andi called me one Monday afternoon as I was getting ready for our weekly dinner. "We're not coming tonight." Her voice sounded thin. "In fact, we're going to take a break for a while. We don't really like the book."

While I already knew Andi and Edward's gripes about the book we were reading at our Monday dinners, I also knew it was not the reason they were backing out.

Edward inched closer to the cause when he gave Pastor Dave a similar call about stepping away from the Inlet as a whole. "You bet on the wrong horse," he said. And when I heard about the call, later, from Dave, I wondered what it meant, beyond his feeling that Dave supported Danny, when, in Edward's view, Joanna was victimized. Because each Sunday Joanna sat sobbing at her table throughout the service while Danny continued to show up, play in the worship band, and now, began dating. All this solidified a strong narrative: Danny abandoned Joanna. And then Andi and Edward left us.

Snap—a connection severed.

But as I saw Dave's support shift from robust to tepid to downright shaky, I wondered if Edward and Andi pulled out too fast. Dave's focus turned to plummeting numbers: fewer youth, smaller offerings, more families leaving the church. More importantly, he spoke of increased criticism from his sons, Matt and Kaleb, a former Inlet member, both at odds not only with Danny but with their father's support of him. I didn't understand then the desperation of a parent who feared losing a son. I'd forgotten how hard it was to advocate for others when your own support structures were shaky. I couldn't see yet how fragile the Inlet was or how quickly it could crumble. I just knew that suddenly, people had stopped embracing Danny.

Snap.

And then, one December evening, I was curled up in my corner of the couch when an email came in from my department head. Shock jolted my system as I absorbed the news. I wasn't going to be teaching my full course load when we came back after the holiday break. The schedule shifted, and she'd reassigned two of my classes to tenured professors.

I'd be teaching a single course in the spring. I barely had a job.

What had I done to my life, my career, my aspirations?

Snap.

29

Shopping Mall Academy

Cynthia

MONSTER, CAREERBUILDER, INDEED.COM—I became an avid consumer of job-posting sites as I hurled myself into the job market, tapping out applications between grading final papers. I loved teaching at Christopher Newport, but adjunct life had defeated me. The educational pickings were slim—mostly postings from the for-profit sector: business and technical schools with names recognizable from daytime television commercials. It wasn't long before I had an interview for a permanent job teaching English at a proprietary college operating out of the upper floors of a large shopping center. I soon found myself planning a teaching demo for a panel of people simply called "management." The day of the interview, I slid into a parking space around the corner from a favorite sandwich chain and a few clothing stores. I tried to stave off a craving for a veggie sub and diverted my gaze from the cute party dresses in the window displays. I was *on campus* now, never mind the lack of columns or fountains or flyers promoting lectures and author talks. I walked through a glass doorway on the side of a Barnes and Noble, up a staircase, and down a hallway flanked by bulletin boards showcasing cardboard cut-outs of snowmen and posters advocating positive outlooks and fresh starts.

I sat in a vinyl chair next to a reception desk and was soon greeted by a plain woman with a neutral palette and a soft voice. She introduced herself as Yvonne, the woman who invited me to interview. She led me down a hallway adorned with near-billboard-sized signs featuring photos and testimonial blurbs from former down-and-outers turned office managers, medical assistants, and jail wardens as a result of their studies. I related to these people on some level—adults who refused to give up on themselves after plans A, B, and C failed, people who wanted something they could count on. On some level I was looking for a new way to be in this world that made sense—a role I could cling to as my elevator pitch for who I was as a human, where I belonged. Having completed or failed at so many past revisions—mother, art teacher, youth leader, reporter, tenure candidate—perhaps, now, hardworking shopping mall instructor could work. It was something I could devote myself to, an identifiable role to play in a school community. Not in scattered piecemeal efforts, scraps stitched together, but a whole, complete career. It could still happen, couldn't it?

We entered a classroom where Yvonne introduced me to two members of the management team who wanted me to delve right into my material. My teaching demo was a mini lesson on opinion writing that involved sampling and rating sandwich cookies. A serious, suit-sporting businessman surprised me by being the only one who played along. After my lesson was over, he asked a few questions about my résumé and then rose to leave. "You're a bit of a fast tracker," he said with a shake of his head. "You may find that you'll need to break things down a bit more for the slower students," he said as he headed to the door, leaving me with Yvonne and another female manager named Roberta.

While I was still considering how an English lesson could become more approachable than listing the pros and cons of a standard sandwich cookie, Roberta turned to me. "Describe the caliber of student you think you will find here."

My mind went immediately to my remedial English class at the Bible college. "I think I will find a lot of people who may not fit well in a traditional college setting," I said.

Roberta peered at me over her glasses. "Yes. But do you know what that means?" she demanded, launching into a catalog of ills: poverty, scammers trying to collect grant money without doing work, single mothers who miss classes for lack of childcare, high school dropouts on their second and third chances—problems that seemed to leave Roberta weary, if not jaded, but piqued my interest and made me excited.

Yvonne returned and led me on a tour around the concrete campus, concentric squares of hallways and classrooms, nested like a set of quadrate babushka dolls.

"We fill a niche," Yvonne was explaining. "We help students that no one else will take."

She opened a door, and I followed her into a pale space with a laden desk surrounded by boxes—her office. "You can get creative," she said, settling into the seat behind the desk. "Take field trips downstairs to Barnes and Noble!"

I wasn't sure if I was horrified or intrigued by the possibility of working in a place—college? school? degree mill?—run by managers and powered by the bottom line. This opportunity in no way resembled the academia I loved, but since that institution was so thoroughly screwing me over, the idea of casting my lot with the second-chancers was growing on me. I related to them. Not likely to garner much respect on the typical academic circuit, Shopping Mall Academy was admittedly on-brand for me. It was time to ask the question—the potential deal-breaker: "Is the position year-round?"

"Yes," Yvonne said. "We have three full semesters. I think there's a week, *maaayy-beee* two between one of them. And Christmas break," she added, a lilt of encouragement in her voice.

"And what's the course load?" I asked, although I was already deflated.

"Full time is six classes per semester. You'll get first pick of all the classes," she assured me, "so you'll get some day classes, not just late nights and weekends. And we really try not to have you here six days a week," she said, her voice a rush of reassurance.

Six classes is a massive workload. Full-time faculty at CNU taught four. I'd done five one semester between both CNU and the Bible school and been reduced to a life of squalor, books and papers teetering in Jenga-like stacks on tables and sofas, dirty and clean laundry intermingling in scattered piles, coffee mugs scattered through the house in a sort of connect-the-dots mapping of my whereabouts. And this wouldn't be for just a season; it wouldn't be a big push toward something bigger, better, or greater. It would be my life. All the time, relentless. I began to absorb what that might look like: stacks of papers in July, workdays that ended at 10:00 p.m. and began anew at 8:00 the next morning, teaching on Saturdays, and all for a salary that might approach what I'd make as a public high school teacher, but no summer. No office. No benefits. No tuition write-off, and an MFA to finish.

It wasn't a viable position, so I asked Yvonne if she had any adjunct work. I still needed a solution, a way forward. I accepted the single class she offered without asking about the compensation, which I'd later discover was just over half of what I made per class at Christopher Newport. And with the addition of Shopping Mall Academy, I was officially back to juggling three different schools—two for meager paychecks that would go straight to the third: Old Dominion, where I was closing in on completing my MFA. Adding Shopping Mall Academy to my schedule was going to bring a lot of extra work into my life for little compensation. Still, I knew the names on my roster were flesh-and-blood humans with goals and dreams and reasons they registered for this class—my class. I wanted to know them and their stories.

I ROLLED OUT OF BED one Saturday in early January to attend what had been described as a two-hour orientation with breakfast. I ascended the staircase and navigated the nesting hallways, now flanked with snowflakes and new-year-new-you-style messages, and filed into a seat at one of two long tables facing a blackboard. A half-empty box of donuts sat next to a carton of juice on the other side of the room. Breakfast. The cookie-eating management team member who'd called me a "fast tracker" at my interview outlined an agenda that would clearly exceed two hours: computer training, breakout sessions, photos, pep talks, and a tour during which everyone gathered in what appeared to be a break room with desks. A wiry man in an argyle sweater directed our attention to a set of shelves containing an endless row of navy-blue binders.

"These are your course binders," he said with an air of reverence. "Every single thing you do must be recorded in these binders. The mother ship can audit these at any time."

A hand shot upward. "What's the mother ship?"

The man in argyle laughed. "That's the name for our main campus up east. Everything we do in this building is delivered from the mother ship."

The rules—edicts apparently handed down by the mother ship—seemed endless: class was never to be canceled, attendance sheets were always delivered to management at the end of class, every interaction with students was to be logged in the blue binder. The mother ship seemed big on paperwork.

I wandered over to the coffee machine where another trainee, a stooped woman with silver hair, stood clutching a handcrafted walking stick, beaming as she took in the scene. "This," she declared, "is worth the drive!"

"Oh?" I said, blinking away my surprise. I was pretty sure I couldn't say the same, and I could be on my couch in under eight minutes. "Where are you coming from?"

She named a southside city accessible only through one of the bridge tunnels, a commute few consider "worth the drive" for anything that doesn't involve a steep benefits package or the ocean. During the morning's introductions, this woman claimed to be teaching ten classes at six institutions. Scanning the rows of shared desks that represented the sum total of faculty office space, the sterile walls, and the conspicuous lack of anything resembling office supplies (BYO), I may have wondered what we had here that the other five institutions lacked, were I not preoccupied with the fear that in this nomadic veteran instructor I'd seen a glimpse of my own future.

AND YET, I HAD DONE what Dr. James deemed impossible—almost. After just three years as an adjunct, I had been actively pursued for a tenure-track position at the Bible college. An unlikely near-success story. Yet here I was, just a year later, cobbling together a set of jobs in an attempt to replace the income from my lost classes. Along with the literature class I still had at CNU and the comp class from the mother ship, I resumed what was typically a summertime, coffee-and-spending-money gig: writing business profiles for a local publication. In the summer, the challenge of making the inner workings of dentists' offices, accounting firms, and lawyers' practices read like grown-up, *Sesame Street*–type "who-are-the-people-in-your-neighborhood" pieces was an amusing diversion. Now, interviews with realtors and shopkeepers were just line items in an ever-growing list of headaches.

I also took a job grading papers for a professor at Old Dominion, even though grading is the aspect of academia for which I am least suited. I will do anything to avoid it: dawdle, procrastinate, toss the whole stack of papers in my trunk. The job was loathsome, but I had tuition to pay—lots of it. Worse, I found the position as shameful as it was burdensome. At least as an adjunct I still could pass as a professional in the outside world. To the general public I was a *professor*, an intellectual, someone with a position of respect. But a grader? Someone who did another professor's grunt work? I couldn't bring myself to admit to anyone that I had plummeted this low. I pictured people shaking their heads, stroking their chins. "She grades papers? I thought she was getting tenure," someone would say. "Nope, she couldn't just keep her mouth shut and sign the paperwork." Everyone would *tsk* in response.

My bitterness grew as I discovered that actually getting paid for grading these papers would become tantamount to another job. Hours vaporized as I completed my tour through the bowels of the ODU payment system. There was a lot of paperwork involved, and, honestly, I am terrible at that too. I'd forget to submit my timesheets, or when I actually did remember, someone else would forget to approve it. Either way, I was left with the legwork if I wanted to see my funds. I began to budget time for collections among my compounding duties.

I used the time traipsing through the accounting department to curse everything that led to my downfall: my trumped-up idealism, an oversensitive moral code, an almost inexplicable loyalty to sexual minorities. What had they ever done for me? Besides, I "supported" lots of people over the years without falling on my own metaphoric sword. I'd had a student with no arms, friends who couldn't eat bread, a child terrified of crickets—and I've supported them all in practical ways: holding doors, baking with oats, reading *A Cricket in Times Square* aloud in a failed desensitization attempt. What had my rejection-of-the-statement stunt accomplished, exactly? Who was benefiting?

My research was hampered. The Old Dominion LGBTQIA+ group had regarded me with suspicion when I asked for their assistance in gathering data for a class. I was hurt, but I understood the difficulty in trusting an outsider. Then Danny announced that Marty would be in town for the weekend and suggested we include him in pizza night. Marty, who had lived in Danny and Joanna's guesthouse as Madi, had fully transitioned, despite his mother's attempts to thwart his efforts.

"You should talk with him about the book. He's got a lot of good stories," Danny said.

It was true. Marty had stories. He was funny and engaging and an all-around asset to pizza night. Then Danny told him about how I was writing his story—my story—our story, and Marty hedged. "It's just that ..." his voice trailed. "We like to tell our own stories."

My heart sank. He didn't see the larger story of what happened when the trajectory of Danny's life intersected with the direction mine was heading. Of how Danny's body and life were so out of line with mainstream Christianity that I—a straight, happily married suburban mother—had been deemed unfit for service by association, by failing to condemn. Of how the church isn't accepting of fresh voices or allies. Or independent thought. He didn't see how Danny was finding his voice at the same time I was finding mine—how the more we advocated for ourselves, for each other, the more the church kept trying to mute us. That I was feeling just a fraction of what Danny had lived with his entire life and it had reduced me to near desperation in a year. I was battling depression, fighting for my MFA, and disillusioned with my faith. That I could hit such a low in a year spoke volumes. And Marty didn't think it was my story.

Maybe I have no idea how to be an ally. The idea jolted me in what felt a lot like another, resounding snap. Did I turn down tenure in exchange for a voice that was destined to be muted?

Highs were hard to come by that miserable winter, but I found a few. I took pride whenever my Fitbit tracker indicated that I exceeded twenty thousand steps. I fell hard for the coffee station at the Shopping Mall Academy—a machine I still regard as a wonder of the modern world. It was taller than me, with large chambers that housed four different types of whole-bean coffee that it would grind on the spot, to the specifications selected on the front screen. Interior chambers stored chocolate and syrups that blended into the fresh brew to make mochas and lattes on demand. I was determined to supplement my income with liberal enjoyment of this solitary perk.

But the chocolaty coffee undoubtedly offset any benefit from the extra mileage my Fitbit logged, resulting in a stagnant break-even that seemed like a metaphor for my whole life. Deadlines began snowballing: photos and copy for who-are-the-people-in-your-neighborhood pieces on Attorney X and Accountant Y, interviews to conduct for the newspaper's next issue, and the grading, the ever-present grading. People began leaving Shopping Mall Academy in droves. A professor, rumored to have a doctorate from an Ivy League school, was found crying in the break room for having her pay, such as it was, docked for an emergency surgery that caused her to cancel a class. At least six other people I trained with were gone by midterm. Yvonne asked me if I wanted more classes.

It should have been an easy no, but I hesitated for a moment as my students' faces flashed across my mind. There was Laura, the older woman with stringy hair and big glasses who relied on public transportation; Gina, the twenty-three-year-old veteran who wrote a persuasive paper against women serving in combat roles and lugged a 120-pound rucksack into class one evening to demonstrate why; Karen B., the stout, middle-aged woman who couldn't operate a computer. Then there was Karen T., a lean woman in her midfifties who introduced herself as a business owner but turned out to just be selling off several rooms' worth of junk she accumulated during a hoarding phase; Kristie, the recent high school graduate who joined us a month into the semester after dropping out of community college; and Amy, the bright, midtwenties woman who aspired to be a lawyer and almost certainly needed to transfer.

Most of all, I thought of Charlene, a slender woman of fifty-four who had failed the course the previous semester. The first night of class she announced she was giving herself six years to get a degree and then she was done. I asked her why she would give up on herself at sixty, and she said if she didn't make it by then, she never would. I could almost hear the clock ticking away at her dreams. Every night she thanked me for helping her, encouraging her, telling her she could do it. And it was her encouragement that told me that maybe I could make it too.

I honestly loved my students. I wanted to help them, but I could barely help myself. Of course, I couldn't take on more classes midsemester: I wasn't even keeping up with what I had. Well-meaning friends were quick to remind me what a good job my husband had, failing to recognize my financial and personal responsibilities: tuitions—mine and my son's—my car payment, and my self-actualization, none of which were being satisfied. The only place I really felt effective, vital, and alive was in my classroom at CNU, presiding over my one remaining class. I was a struggling adjunct—the thing no one aspires to be.

I came in the door from class one night and fell into Brad's arms in gasping sobs. "I am so unhappy."

30
The Wedding

Danny

I STOOD IN FRONT OF the trellis where, in a couple hours, I'd be exchanging vows with Krista. But not like this. Something was just plain wrong. I'm no art expert, but it was clear that someone else was going to have to arrange the flowers around those beams and through those holes because, at the moment, the trellis looked like a kindergarten craft—stems here, limp buds there.

All I truly cared about was the moment we'd stand there becoming husband and wife, but the trellis was important to Krista and I wanted this day to be everything we planned it to be. And, honestly, this trellis was going to hold a lot of memories for me too. We were about to stand right here, among my sister Barb's handmade silk flowers, while my brother Jim pronounced us man and wife in front of friends and family. My oldest brothers, Rick and Bill, and my sister Mary, who, as our mistress of ceremonies was the glue holding this day together, would soon sit in the white folding chairs on the lawn behind me. The trellis was where my father, Ben, would say a prayer of blessing right before we'd say our vows. It's where Krista and I would take a first communion together with my mom and dad. In front of the purples, whites, and pops of orange around this trellis, I would do the one thing I never dreamed possible: marry the love of my life, in public, as a man—with the support of my entire family.

"Hey! We've got this!" I turned as Cynthia and Allison approached the trellis.

"Oh my goodness!" My face broke into a smile as the words came out in a gush of relief. "You have the time?

"Our hair and makeup are done and I'd way rather be out here than up in the dressing area right now." Cynthia began picking flowers from the cardboard box and threading them around the trellis. "Go on, go do your things—we've got this."

And I knew she did.

❧～❧

I SLID OUT OF THE room where Brad, my best man; and my groomsmen, Brandon, Marty, Krista's brother, and two other friends, were tying ties and snapping cufflinks. Krista met me in the hall, neither of us dressed yet in wedding attire. We were stealing one last moment before becoming husband and wife to exchange gifts. *I am marrying the girl of my dreams,* I thought as I opened the small package Krista slipped into my hands. My heart jumped as I realized it was a pocket watch—one I had admired and really wanted, but now it was engraved with the words "Until the End of Time" with our wedding date inscribed beneath.

Until the end of time. That's all I wanted—someone to go forward with *me*—as my true self, as the person I was finally able to be.

As though she was reading my thoughts, Krista looked me in the eyes and said, "I love you for who you are. I am so excited that I get to be your wife."

I handed my package to Krista. It was a time marker of sorts too: a bound photo book with pictures a friend had taken for us. I wrote captions for each page—all different ways of expressing my love, my trust, my excitement to begin our lives together.

So many impossible things happened that day. I got married legally, as a man. I had a real wedding—not a trumped-up birthday party, but an actual ceremony with friends from my past, colleagues, and my entire family. I danced with my mother. Marty was there as a groomsman, and many people at the reception—in the wedding party, even—didn't know either of our pasts. Krista and I approached the entry to the shelter where friends and family, dinner and dancing, cake and crisp white wine were waiting. I spread both arms out and crossed the threshold, into my future, ready to receive all of it with arms wide open.

31

Things Worth Toasting

Cynthia

BRAD STOOD WITH DANNY AND Krista near the cake, holding a glass in one hand and a microphone in the other. "This day marks the beginning of a new adventure. I say *adventure* because the best parts in life are those you don't see coming. An adventure is only an adventure when things don't go as planned. Our best memories and the stories we tell most often are always of things that went wrong—the short-term disasters that turned out okay in the end."

For a quiet man, Brad has a knack for pulling out the right words in clutch situations. Our shared philosophy about adventure is something of a motto we live by, and a perfect opening for his wedding toast. It was the hottest day of the year, an absolutely smoldering day for an outdoor wedding. I know Brad would have been happier wearing anything other than the full suit he was in, but I was secretly happy. My man looked incredible.

"Knowing Danny, there will be no lack of short-term disasters. And knowing God, things will always turn out okay in the end. You two are in for quite an adventure. Whether it's melting the church's folding table with his charcoal grill or letting my dog lick what's left of his dinner off his shirt, there is always something going on with Danny that isn't quite what we thought would happen." Brad paused until the ripple of laughter subsided. "Despite the ongoing struggle, he remains the most confident, upbeat, and positive person I know—and other than my wife and kids, Danny has had a more profound impact on my view of the world than anyone, and I am truly blessed to have him as my friend."

In this I agree with my husband wholeheartedly. Danny taught me that deciding to be yourself is the bravest thing anyone can ever do. He taught me the importance of living in a state of harmony, of making sure your insides and outsides match. For people like Danny, the costs of coming out, of stepping into your own identity, are astronomical; the risks are literally life and death. But Danny also taught me that you don't have to be intersex to have a "coming out" experience. The one thing all of us—gay, straight, male, female, conservative, liberal, and on the continuum between the absolutes—have in common is the fear that we won't be accepted. The fear of what we'll lose if we are "known."

Danny lived his life under this shadow that to be known would mean to be discarded, and then he taught me to let go of that fear. The day I channeled his coming-out speech in the university boardroom was my own "coming out." It was the moment I chose to be me despite the consequences. The moment I realized that an opportunity lost to the truth was never mine in the first place. It was the moment I chose to be known instead of liked. It was also the instant I went from giving lip service to allyship to living it out in real time. Although I still wondered from time to time if I knew how to be an effective ally, at the rehearsal dinner the night before, I realized the concern might be mine alone: Marty wasn't thinking that way. Not now, perhaps not ever.

"How's the book coming?" he asked, as he slid into an empty seat near Brad and me at one of the tables in the back room of the pizza shop where we'd gathered. I tried to suppress my shock as I filled him in on the latest. He seemed invested, interested. And at that moment, another story line seemed to resolve.

Watching Danny dance with his mother at his wedding, I remembered the evening he left my house to tell his parents the truth. That night they had been asked, in the course of an hour, to edit the story of their lives—the entire narrative of their sixth and last child. Forty-plus years of birthdays, holidays, and events both mundane and milestone—shattered. They were thrown into a maelstrom of cognitive dissonance. Immutable tenets of their conservative belief system had been challenged and pitted against the strength of the parent-child bond. And they rose to that challenge. Here they were, as a family, supporting Danny in a way his younger self would have never imagined possible: as a man, marrying the girl of his dreams. And that's the thing about lines: they can be erased. We can reexamine absolutes, rules, principles, dogma against new information. We can expand and make room for new thought, new ways to include more people, more life.

This, Danny and Krista's wedding day, was in many ways the culmination of a miracle. It was a story of bravery, identity, truth. If, as Brad suggested in his toast, an adventure is something you don't see coming, then my family had been part of a huge one over the two years since Danny read his script to Brad and me across a Panera table. It was an adventure I would sign up for every time. It may have cost me a career, an office, and a windfall, but it sharpened my confidence, strengthened my sense of self, and increased the number of people I call family. That was a win I could toast.

"May you embrace the adventure set before you," Brad said.

I did. I will. Glasses shot upward around me.

"To a lifetime of love, happiness, and things going wrong but being awesome anyway."

Brad's words were true and beautiful, especially delivered to the soundtrack of a couple hundred clinking glasses.

Epilogue

Cynthia

"I'm at cici's desk! I'm doing work!"

My heart expands as it always does at the shrill tones radiating from the three-year-old tumble of curls and energy perched in my university office chair.

I pour a few tablespoons of water around my succulents, enough, I estimate, to see them through the handful of days until I return. The spring semester ended a week ago, but I know I'll be in and out between now and fall—to have lunch with Allie, our new office manager, or to repeat the errand I'm on today, grabbing a carton of pastel eggs from Nick, the religion and philosophy professor down the hall. Nick—or Hippie Nicky, as I hear students affectionately call him—brings in eggs from his chicken coop every couple of weeks, and I want that pop of color and freshness in my life and on my plate, even in the academic off-season. I'll be back also, at some point, to pick up Emma and Ashley, students from my fall nonfiction workshop, for the dinner I promised to stave off the loneliness of a summer-session campus. There's also a good chance that I'll return to my office over the summer just to write, to break a bit from the din of a home that still hums with activity—Brad and me, our dogs, and the toddler I'm now steering out my office door.

I am still teaching at Christopher Newport. I am still an adjunct, but a pretty happy one. A lot about my circumstances hasn't changed, but yet everything is different. *I* am different. Before I close the door on my office, I look back at the framed art prints I've placed around the room, getting a feel for where it all should go. I make a mental note to put in a work order to have them hung, and I close the door—for now. The nameplate mounted in the hall next to my door remains empty. My name won't be engraved and displayed outside, but I have made a whole world on the other side of the door. My office is a kind of open secret, a thing we know in our department but don't advertise on placards. Accordingly, the gatherings I'll host in the post-pandemic future will be more like speakeasies than happy hours, but I cannot wait to hold them.

These days, I don't lose quite as many classes to tenured faculty because completing my MFA has allowed me to teach upper-level and specialty courses. I'm developing a journalism class for next spring that I am uniquely qualified to teach. Although my MFA afforded me the opportunity to teach meatier courses, I began to truly make a professional home for myself when I found my voice.

One day last August, when pandemic conditions highlighted inequalities across the board in our country, I began talking about life as an adjunct— first on a faculty thread, then in our faculty senate, and, ultimately, in a state-wide organizational meeting. I found allies, for sure; but, more importantly, I began to find friends—to be known.

As an adjunct I taught face-to-face throughout the pandemic, denied by administration the opportunity to settle into an online teaching role—an option many full-time, tenured faculty enjoyed. I was gifted an office as a concession, and I recently learned I will be permitted to keep it.

❧❧

WHEN LINES INTERSECT, THEY SHARE a common point—a space of impact. Was it a coincidence that Danny's path met mine the moment he ended his masquerade and the instant I could have donned my own life of pretense? Was our discussion that night across the Panera booth no more or less than a pact to live authentically?

I had no idea, of course, what consequences would come of that decision—or if there would even be any. I didn't know the winter of 2016, when I fought and scraped to replace the income from my lost classes, to pay my tuition, to keep my safety net intact, was just the moment sparks of trouble caught oxygen. My life hadn't even begun to burn. That year, flames were licking around the edges of my faith, my family, and my fears, but the fire was in its early stages—not fully developed. At that time I was still trying to keep my safety net together—to stitch up the holes and force it to remain in service.

The initial sparks ignited when I lost the professorship, but it was just the beginning of my awareness of the instability of all I once considered bedrock. Ugly, dangerous lines were beginning to shift the foundation, the underpinning of what was supposed to be the strongest community of all: my Christian faith. That same year Danny and Krista married, the political climate shifted, and the crack widened and went so deep as to seem irreparable. The version of Christianity I saw playing out in the political arena matched nothing inside of me. Communities were crumbling everywhere I turned.

When I first wrote about my former youth group member Steve, I knew I needed to attend to some wounds I caused too. It didn't take much to find him on social media, and I didn't hesitate to send him a message once I did. I honestly wasn't sure how much of that brief discussion he remembered, or if it bothered him as much as I feared it had. He responded immediately and compassionately, questioning me about my personal journey and accepting my apology. He shared our exchange on social media, and one of the first people to comment was his mother, who I had never met. If I'd had any doubt about the impact of the conversation on Steve's life, her words erased it. She remembered the day well. She expressed grudging happiness that I had apologized but stated, "I'm glad I never treated you like that." Okay; I guess I had that coming.

Peters stepped down as president of the Bible college. Jim, the sole administrator at that boardroom table who seemed genuinely interested in learning about intersex and insisted that he'd want to read my book, replaced him at the helm. To date, there has been no recantation of the Family and Marriage Statement, but I just might send Jim a copy of this manuscript one fine day when it's in print.

Danny tried to stay in Momma Miller's life. He was initially successful in working with Joanna to carve out a weekly visitation with her, but eventually she asked him to stop coming. Momma Miller was diagnosed with a terminal respiratory disease, and when she passed away three years after Danny moved out, Joanna was true to her word: she barred Danny from attending the funeral.

Brad and I pitched in and tried to help revive the once-vibrant youth group at the Inlet, but it dwindled first to a half-dozen teens, then two or three, until, finally, no one showed at all. Our entire network of friends—a few members of our weekly dinner group, Rob the Customer, three or four delightful, open-minded couples we enjoyed—left one by one for reasons that ranged from moves to discontent. Brandon graduated from college and stepped down as the music minister. I tried to choke back the tears his final Sunday, but once they started to come, they didn't stop. I knew it was the end of an era for our family in that community. Allison had already resigned as the children's minister and had a foot out the door. Danny, Krista, Brad, and I were pretty much the odd people out in a congregation that was swinging increasingly conservative.

The last thing we did at the Inlet was take a single youth group member to Haiti the following summer. We did some scrappy, hardscrabble fundraisers and tried to repeat the art auction that had been so successful the year before, when the Inlet just wanted to help Brandon and me go on our own. But the auction went largely unsupported by the church. Gorgeous pieces of art sat on display for weeks behind empty bid sheets. We were being shunned.

By then, I liked church even less than I had the previous year when the Haitian woman asked us to pray that she would like church. This trip, with Danny, Krista, and our lone youth group member, was hard. Since there were so few of us, the organization we went with teamed us up with a conservative group that made no effort to hide their contempt for our small band of outsiders. That trip, my sixth, was also my first time there without my son, who was going through his own crisis of life and faith and was becoming increasingly distant.

That year wasn't all bad, though: Tyler, Allison's high school friend and my bonus son, got engaged to Sonny, a warm, funny, and thoughtful man. They got married in Germany. Allison and I flew to Europe for the wedding along with Tyler's entire family. The wedding was a twelve-hour party in a barn in the German countryside. A DJ from Amsterdam spun tracks until the early morning hours. No one danced longer, harder, or with more enthusiasm than his father, Ray.

Weeks after we returned from Europe, Brad and I received the unexpected news that would ultimately save us: our daughter was pregnant.

Because, by then, the fire that caught eighteen months earlier was fully developed, raging. We had no church, I was resentful of my career, and my son was falling further from our lives all the time. Allison's baby wasn't even a year old when Brandon crossed the threshold of our home for the last time, shutting the door on our family, the most stable and precious community I had ever known.

Life as I knew it was over, consumed, burned to the cracked foundation. For a season, the landscape of my life resembled the images I saw on the news in the wake of the California wildfires: scorched, ruined, communities turned to ash and dust, the remains taken by the wind. All the communities I have joined or made are gone, lost to time or damage: the round church, the teen girls Bible study, the elementary school, the Inlet, and now the unthinkable: the family I idolized.

How many versions of myself have been lost in the ashes?

Brad and I had each other, our daughter, and her baby, who filled me with more joy than I thought possible. We also had our friendship with Danny and Krista that came with a renewed pact to be a safe space for each other—a place to shelter while we waited to see what new life would spring from the scarred earth. What happened, though, was a pandemic. A global crisis that laid the world bare. A time that shuttered churches and formed cracks through which truths would emerge anyway. A time of silence that birthed reckonings and realizations.

❧

MY PHONE LIT UP ONE day with a text from a friend I met as a teen at the round church, someone who had woven in and out of my life for twenty years but had been largely gone for some time after joining an insular, conservative church several years ago.

She was going by a different name than the one I knew her by, but that wasn't all she had to tell me.

The trio of bubbles promising a pending text danced on my phone for an inordinate amount of time, but I instinctively knew what was coming.

The long scroll that finally popped on my screen recounted her version of life laid bare: lockdown, solitude, a voice she recognized as her own whispering truth that would cost her everything.

"I'm gay," she typed. "And I can't go back to church."

A one-line addendum popped up. "Also, I'm vegan."

I paused for a moment, smiling as my thumbs banged out my response: "Vegan?? WOW. What happened?"

<hr />

"You can never be you," Reese, who now used they/them pronouns, was saying. Although I had introduced Reese to Danny and Krista and they'd joined our growing home pod immediately after coming back into my life, we were finally vaccinated and out at a brewery, enjoying a taste of post-pandemic life.

"It's like a construct of you, but you're forcing yourself into a box." Reese paused. "Being myself was unacceptable. So I doubled down, determined that I could make myself acceptable, but eventually—it seemed like death would be better. Religion shouldn't make you want to kill yourself," they said.

I paused for a moment, conjuring an old memory. "Do you remember when I stole the puppet?"

They laughed and nodded. "I remember some of that," they said. "It was a long time ago."

"A really long time," I agreed. "But I remember doing it like it was yesterday because I get what you're saying. What I saw that week at camp was the church focusing on such a small percentage of the people there. It made me angry. Church is supposed to be about inclusion—it should be for everyone. But too many people land on the margins too much of the time. Sexual minorities, women, people with broad views on scripture..."

It hit me later, as I reflected on our conversation, how many times my own view of community was less than inclusive. How communities are networks of people colliding at myriad intersections every day. How those points of connection can be happy accidents or tragic collisions. How intersections can be places of near misses, chance encounters, or spaces where things bump and graze. Where split-second decisions can have life-and-death consequences. And sometimes? An intersection is just a point to pass through on a journey to somewhere else.

All my life I've craved stable, solid, accepting community—bedrock spaces to which I can always return, places where I am fully known and accepted. I'm trying now to broaden my construct of community. To embrace the idea that communities aren't for me to find, but to build. On some level that's what I have been trying to do all along, but in a flawed, self-serving way. I see now that enjoying a community is a happy by-product, a side effect of building community for others. It's the result of *being a* safe space: my most authentic self embracing your most authentic self, enjoying connection at that intersection, in that moment. Communities are made in the here and now, created in the act of loving what is close at hand, available, in reach.

But communities are also places you can return to. Safe and stable places you can always find, that you know are just a call or a text away. Places to connect and reconnect. Places where you are known. I am going to be that place for others, even as I continue to keep the door open on the possibility of finding a truly inclusive spiritual community. I may one day return to enjoying church from the inside, but for now, I remain committed to living it with those who remain on the outside.

For now, that means dinners and game nights with Danny and Krista and sometimes Reese, and recently, the wonderful woman they've been dating. If we're really lucky, we get my friend Lisa, who began to spend frequent weekends with Brad and me during the pandemic. Sometimes my friend Caroline, who stopped going to church around the time I did, will fold into one of our activities. Danny and Krista and Brad and I have witnessed one another's lowest lows and highest highs. There's no pressure to put on a front, make an excuse, or dodge a question. It's a relatively new experience for all of us, but we're excited to share what we're building. Authentic living is addictive. Now that I've experienced it, I refuse to settle for anything less.

Danny taught me that being known is worth fighting for. It's worth betting everything on. It's risky. It's terrifying. But it's the only thing that matters. I don't have all the answers, but what I do know is, for the rest of my life, anyplace I go—church, job, or otherwise—it will be as me, authentically: insides and outsides all in alignment.

Acknowledgments

THIS BOOK IS ONLY POSSIBLE because of my friend Danny's willingness to spend countless hours in honest, transparent, and, at times, painful reflection of some of the darkest moments of his life. The time he spent reliving his past was a selfless gift offered in hope of a more accepting future. May his story be read as a gift, accepted in love, and considered a call to action.

I am grateful to my family, who allowed me to turn them into literary characters. I especially want to thank my husband, Brad, who, next to Danny, is the person most responsible for what follows—from the initial idea through every rewrite and the long path to publication; his influence is on each and every page.

I would be remiss not to acknowledge my father, George, for modeling faith as an evolving process and for fully supporting not only this book but where I am in my spiritual journey. Thank you, Dad, for your continued affirmation of me and my work.

Thank you, Krista, for entering the story (at least my telling of it) in medias res and not only tolerating it but embracing the project and all that came with it—and becoming family along the way. Thanks also to my friends Lisa, Caroline, Patti, Tracy, Reese, Melissa, Lily; my sister, Emmie; and my friends in the Quarantine Writers Club for cheering me on through every step of this process. Thank you to my Sisters of Perpetual Disorder, Virginia and Anna, for becoming my work community, my colleagues, and—most importantly—treasured friends, who ruined ten years of lurking in hallways and drinking coffee alone with picnics, emergency coffee, a strong GIF game, and various post-work shenanigans. Thank you to Kerry for going through the MFA and post-grad publishing adventure alongside me. Your book is next!

I am appreciative to Joe Jackson, whose stint as a visiting writer at Old Dominion University happily coincided with the second—and better—half of my MFA work. Joe's hard-hitting commentary, evening round tables at Stella's with Kerry, and belief in my story shaped my early iterations of *Intersexion* and, even more importantly, my belief in myself as a writer.

I also wish to acknowledge Kathy Ver Eecke and the Pitch to Published community for teaching me how to pitch my work and for connecting me to my editor, Jessie Stover, who worked with me to shape my manuscript into a polished final project that sizzles so much more than its earlier versions.

And finally, thank you, David Morris, for seeing the potential in my book and in my writing career. Thank you for giving this project such careful attention, bringing in a top-notch support team, and assigning me the incomparable Jenn McNeil as my copy editor. I am so excited to be working on this project with you through Lake Drive. I cannot imagine a better partner for this publishing adventure.

Notes

Chapter 13: Party Lines

At this point, I didn't know about Cameron's ... organization's classification as a hate group with the Southern Poverty Law Center. This information is taken from the article "Paul Cameron: Extremist Info," Southern Poverty Law Center, https://www.splcenter.org/fighting-hate/extremist-files/individual/paul-cameron, accessed 4/1/2022, and https://cpa.ca/aboutcpa/policystatements/#cameron, accessed 4/1/2022.

I hadn't read his interview in Rolling Stone *where he stated: "Marital sex tends toward the boring end. Generally, it doesn't deliver the kind of sheer sexual pleasure that homosexual sex does . . . if all you want is the most satisfying orgasm you can get, then homosexuality seems too powerful to resist."* "Paul Cameron: Extremist Info," https://www.splcenter.org/fighting-hate/extremist-files/individual/paul-cameron, accessed 4/1/2022. The interview can also be found in Robert Dreyfuss, "The Holy War on Gays," *Rolling Stone*, March 18, 1999, Issue 808, p. 38.

About the Author

CYNTHIA VACCA DAVIS TEACHES NARRATIVE nonfiction and journalism at Christopher Newport University. She holds an MFA in creative nonfiction and has led nonfiction workshops at The Muse Writers Center in Norfolk, Virginia, one of the biggest community writing centers of its kind in the country. She's written hundreds of feature stories and profiles, a handful of pieces for literary journals, and two independently published YA novels, *The Chrysalis* and *Drink the Rain*.

When she's not home in coastal Virginia with her husband, pets, and students, she can often be found in the French Quarter of New Orleans in search of jazz and parades. A connoisseur of beverages, she loves to share a cup of just about anything around a table full of friends. Subscribe to her newsletter at cynthiavaccadavis.com or follow her on Twitter @_cynthiadavis and Instagram @cynthia_vacca_davis.

9 781957 687063